# THE AUTHOR

Over 25 years Daniel Taylor's affinity with Nottingham Forest has seen him progress from the Colwick Road terraces to the lower tier of the Executive Stand to the press box. He has been a sportswriter for the *Guardian* since 1999, predominantly covering Manchester United and England. He started his career at the *Newark and South Notts Advertiser* before working as a freelance journalist for several titles, including the *Observer*, the *Daily Mirror* and the *Sunday Times*. He grew up in the Nottinghamshire village of Sibthorpe but now lives in Manchester.

# Deep into the Forest

By Daniel Taylor

**The Parrs Wood Press**
**Manchester**

**First Published 2005**

**THE PARRS WOOD PRESS**
St Wilfrid's Enterprise Centre
Royce Road, Manchester, M15 5BJ
www.parrswoodpress.com

© Daniel Taylor 2005

**ISBN: 1 903158 61 3**

Printed by Compass Press Ltd of London

DEDICATED TO BRIAN CLOUGH,
1935 - 2004, RIP.

The author would also like to thank: Pauline Taylor, James Taylor, Zoe Hall, Matt Appleby, Ben Clissitt, Ian Edwards, Fraser Nicholson, Paul Tyrrell, Tony Mancini, Andy Searle and everyone at Parrs Wood Press.

Photographs courtesy of the *Guardian* newspaper, Eamonn McCabe, Mike King, Frank Baron and Phil Meakin of the *Nottingham Evening Post*.

# CONTENTS

# INTRODUCTION

*In an era when mediocrity is idolised
here stood true genius.*

**Anon. The City Ground gates. September 20th, 2004.**

THE INITIAL PLAN had been to ask Brian Clough to write the foreword. Instead I would like to dedicate this book in his honour. Nostalgia is the file that smoothes the rough edges from the good old days and, thanks to Clough, Forest's supporters will always hold their heads up high when declaring where their affinity lies.

The outpouring of grief that followed Clough's death will be remembered as acutely in future years as the achievements of his teams and, unsurprisingly, he features heavily in every chapter. All but one of the 14 players telling their individual stories have first-hand experience of his unique brand of management. One is his son, Nigel. The exception is Ian Storey-Moore, whom Clough regarded as "the one that got away", having infamously tried to sign him during his time as Derby County's manager. All 14 have undeniable claims to take their place in a collection of Forest greats because of the way they won the affections of the fans and helped to define the club's history, from Manchester to Munich, Coventry to Cologne, Liverpool to London Road.

Yet this is not meant to be the definitive list of City Ground legends. How, for example, can you omit Bob McKinlay, who made his debut in 1951 and was still turning out at the City Ground in 1969, making more appearances for the club than other player in history? Or some of his celebrated teammates, formidable players such as Henry Newton, Frank Wignall and Terry Hennessey? Joe Baker would have been an automatic choice had he still been with us today, as would Jack Burkitt, Forest's last FA Cup-winning captain. Older followers will have fond memories of Wally Ardron's prolific forward play in the 1950s. Duncan McKenzie is worthy of an honourable mention for his goal-scoring exploits in the early-1970s and from more recent years Steve Hodge, Peter

Davenport, Johnny Metgod, Steve Stone and Colin Cooper will always be guaranteed a warm welcome at the City Ground. Equally, the controversial departures of Stan Collymore, Lars Bohinen and Pierre van Hooijdonk does not alter the fact they were among the most naturally talented footballers ever to wear the famous red jersey.

When it comes to the 'glory years' apologies are due to the likes of Martin O'Neill, Ian Bowyer, Frank Clark, Peter Shilton and Tony Woodcock, all of whose names are still revered in Nottingham. Clough might have had something to say about that lot being left out. As it is, the European Cup-winning teams are well represented with Trevor Francis, John McGovern, Viv Anderson, Garry Birtles, Kenny Burns, Archie Gemmill, Larry Lloyd and John Robertson all giving their accounts from that magical period from 1977 to 1980 when a brow slowly crossed the furrow of the football world and Forest won promotion, the league and the European Cup. Twice.

Stuart Pearce, Des Walker, Neil Webb and Nigel Clough were mandatory picks because of the way they illuminated the City Ground in Brian Clough's 'second' Forest team, one that reached Wembley six times in four seasons. Roy Keane made the cut because of his truly outstanding displays during his three years in Nottingham while Storey-Moore represents that great 1966/67 side who came so close to the 'Double', finishing as runners-up to Manchester United in the league and losing to Tottenham Hotspur in the FA Cup semi-finals.

Invariably, they were more generous with their time than I could ever have hoped for. I wanted to know whether, like the rest of us, they really cared for the club. Did they hurt as much as the supporters when things went wrong? Or was it just a day job? Did they think of Nottingham as A. L. Rowse's "magnificent city full of improbable splendours"? Or did they agree with Bryan Roy that "all Nottingham has is Robin Hood, and he's dead"?

Sometimes, of course, a club can be so pre-occupied with years gone by that it allows the past to cloud the future. Joe Kinnear certainly thought as much when he arrived at the City Ground in February 2004. "I see they don't have any pictures of the relegation teams," he cackled a couple of weeks into the job, waving a dismissive hand at the photographs of the European Cup teams on the walls of the pressroom. "Ever since I've been at this club I've had the history rammed down my throat."

He was correct in some respects. Yet the legends on those walls are the same guys who give us hope for the future. That one day there will be another Robertson, another Francis or another Walker. There will never be another Clough, of course. But thanks to the players in this book, and a manager who went by the name of Old Big 'Ead, we can all live in hope in humdrum times. And, for that, we should be eternally grateful.

**Daniel Taylor**
**January 2005**

# ONE

# Stuart Pearce

*My captain would walk through*
*a plate-glass window for this club.*

**Brian Clough**

ERIC CANTONA WAS once asked whether Manchester United still had a place in his heart. "Manchester United doesn't have a place in my heart," replied Old Trafford's *enfant terrible*. "Manchester United is my heart."

There are times in Stuart Pearce's company when you get the feeling he wishes he had thought of that line first - or a Nottingham Forest variation of it, anyway.

"No disrespect to Derby," he says, "but I have to say I could never work for that club in any capacity. And I mean *never*. People might say I'm being ridiculous but that's just the way it is. Even if I was desperate and they were the only club around, I couldn't do it. I'd rather go on the dole and take my chances."

Pearce is stretched out on a sofa at Manchester City's otherwise deserted training ground, wiping the sleep from his eyes. As usual, he is the first to arrive for work. Not even the cleaners have checked in yet but Pearce, the ultimate professional, was out of bed at 6.30a.m. and behind the wheel of his car with his hair still wet from his morning shower. It is typical Pearce. Total and utter commitment.

Forest have been blessed with some great players over the years, from multimillion-pound signings and fancy foreigners to bargain-basement buys and home-grown heroes. In fact, the problem writing this book was deciding which players to leave out. But it is difficult to think of anyone who has come even close to having the same rapport with the supporters as the man who was universally known as 'Psycho'.

# DEEP INTO THE FOREST

This is a man whose testimonial match attracted nearly 3,000 more fans than an FA Cup quarter-final against Aston Villa and whose cult status means he cannot even return to Nottingham for a book-signing session without it descending into chaos. When he brought his autobiography to the club shop in 2000 the queue snaked along Pavilion Road, past the 'greasy spoon' where Brian Clough's European Cup-winners used to get their lunchtime fry-ups and across Trent Bridge. The police were scared it would create a traffic hazard.

Whole rainforests could be lost in analysing the reasons for his popularity. First and foremost, it was his immense talent, the bone-jarring tackles, the lung-splitting surges, the rocket free-kicks and the vein-popping, fists-clenched 'Psycho' salutes that made him, without question, the most formidable left-back of his generation. There would be times when a game had gone flat and he had the knack to inspire the entire crowd single-handedly. A Pearce tackle could send the decibel level soaring. One of those rampaging runs could lift the most mild-mannered spectator from their seat. Suddenly the fans would be singing again and the team would be reinvigorated.

But there was more to it than that. Pearce's charm was his stubborn refusal to be seduced by the bags of gold that football deposited into his bank account. He is a man of uncommon ability yet common views. Winning, he says, is all that ever mattered. The rest, as Harvey Keitel put it in *Mean Streets*, is bullshit. And Pearce belongs firmly to the the-rest-is-bullshit school.

While his teammates gelled their hair, dressed in their designer labels and parked their dream machines, Pearce was happy with a wedged side-parting, a battered old denim jacket and his black, two-litre Ford Capri ("what a car - shame the bottom fell out"). An electrician by trade, in his first two seasons at Forest the one-time Brent Council employee fixed Clough's toaster and even advertised in the centre pages of the match programme: 'Stuart Pearce, Electrician. Complete Household Rewires. Estimates Free. Repairs and Maintenance. All Work Guaranteed. Telephone: 0602 847224.'

"A Brighton fan rang me one morning," he recalls. "He was an electrician as well and we'd played them the night before. He just

14

couldn't believe it was my number in the programme. It made his day."

More than anything, of course, it was his devotion to Forest that endeared him to the supporters. There were times, indeed, when his Michael Caine accent was the only reminder he was born in West London rather than West Bridgford.

"Away at Derby used to be the highlight of the season for me. I used to walk out at the Baseball Ground and give their fans a little girlie wave. Then it would be over to the Forest fans to give them a proper salute. I'd do the same in front of the Kop at Anfield as well - just to stoke up that little extra bit of ill feeling, you understand? There would be old women at Derby shouting and screaming at me, coins landing round my feet and people spitting at me whenever I turned my back to take a throw-in. Christ, they bloody hated me. But, for me, that's what football's all about.

"I would think: 'Yeah, that's right, give me as good as you can - I'm representing that lot in the corner over there.' Honestly, I used to love nothing more than walking out at a ground when you knew everyone hated your guts."

His is a loyalty that has gone out of fashion in an era when a player will kiss his shirt then slap in a transfer request the next day. Pearce turned down Manchester United and Glasgow Rangers to stay at the City Ground and was even willing to jeopardise his England career by dropping down a division once Forest's toes had been tagged for the relegation morgue in 1993.

Post-Premiership, would he wind down? Like hell. Pearce was tremendous the following season. It was only fitting he should head in the second goal in the 3-2 victory that won Frank Clark's team promotion at Peterborough and it was typical he was the last player to leave the red whirlpool that engulfed the pitch after the final whistle.

The fans had been scaling the walls and the floodlights of London Road that day and Stan Collymore's 88th-minute winner set off the first of two mass pitch invasions. Pearce even helped the police horses and Alsatians to help restore a few minutes of peace and order before the final whistle set off another stampede.

"It wasn't a problem," he says. "Yeah, I was mobbed but it was just like being down Rock City. Except I didn't get spat on."

Hypothetical, of course, but how different it might have been if Manchester United had had their way. In the days when Sir Alex Ferguson was just a plain old Mister he was so desperate to sign the future England captain he and his chairman Martin Edwards drove to the City Ground "on a whim" and bowled into the reception asking to see Brian Clough.

It was their bad luck to find Clough in one of his more obstinate moods. Whereas most managers would have dropped everything at hearing Ferguson was at the door, Old Green Jersey kept him outside for hours before sending a message that he would not be coming out at all. Like it or lump it.

In his autobiography, *Managing My Life*, a chastened Ferguson recalls Pearce was "a player I had long coveted, one whose courage, confidence in his own ability and competitive temperament suggested he would be an ideal wearer of United's colours."

Spending a fruitless afternoon in the City Ground car park was not the sort of treatment to which Ferguson was accustomed and he concludes: "Brian Clough provided ample proof that he was one of British football's greatest managers. That he was almost certainly its rudest is another distinction he is proud to claim. He is welcome to it."

Ferguson accusing Clough of being ill-mannered is a bit like Dennis Wise complaining about a late tackle. Forest's version of events was that Ferguson had a cheek turning up without even a courtesy call. And Pearce is happy to put the record straight anyway.

"I've never regretted it once. Bryan Robson had told me when we were away with England that Ferguson wanted to sign me but I was happy at Forest. I was in the England squad, loving where I lived and enjoying playing for the man I worked for.

"I was mid-contract anyway and to go into Brian Clough's office and tell him you'd love to join Manchester United . . . well, you could do that if you wanted a life of hell.

"I'm a pretty loyal fellow and I knew how much Forest had done for me. So I had no reason to want to leave. And once I'd made that decision I never looked back. I've seen a similar thing happen to other players who ended up sulking with their club, but that was never the case with me.

"Besides, you have to bear in mind that Forest were winning things at that time whereas Manchester United weren't. We'd won a couple of League Cups, been in back-to-back semi-finals of the FA Cup and finished third in the league in successive seasons, so we were a team on the rise. There was only Liverpool at the time who were better than us and it was a thin line."

Ah, Liverpool. Pearce's views on Derby might seem conservative compared to some of the vitriol that might be unleashed were the tape recorder to be paused. His was a grudge that stemmed not only from the bitter rivalry between the two clubs in the late-80s but from his knowledge that Liverpool were not just a superior team but a more cynical one, too - one whose ethos could have been derived from Stephen Potter's *Gamesmanship or the Art of Winning Games Without Actually Cheating*.

Pearce will never forget, for instance, the way in which John Aldridge ruffled Brian Laws's hair in mock congratulations ("I would have chinned him") after he scored an own-goal in the post-Hillsborough FA Cup semi-final replay at Old Trafford.

His dislike of Steve McMahon, Liverpool's regulation hatchet man, was even more intense, boiling over one day while on England duty. "We had a big row and got involved in something stupid," he recalls. "It was the end of the 1988/89 season and they had stopped us getting to the FA Cup final again. I'm not proud of it but it all boiled down to my frustration that they kept beating us.

"For a couple of years I had a passionate dislike of Liverpool. I'm not going to apologise for it but if I'm being truly honest it was probably jealousy on my part because we couldn't beat them.

"I'm the kind of guy who wants to win at all costs and, Christ, it hurts to say it, but they were always better than us. If you'd put John Barnes and Peter Beardsley in our team, maybe it would have tipped the balance. But they were a cut above us at that time. They dumped us out of two FA Cup semi-finals and I'm convinced if we had played anybody else we would have been good enough to get into the final."

# DEEP INTO THE FOREST

After 522 games for the club, a period in which he won 76 of his 78 England caps and scored 88 of his 99 career goals, it seems faintly ridiculous now that Pearce was actually considered the makeweight in the £450,000 deal that saw him and Ian Butterworth arrive from Coventry City in the summer of 1985.

Butterworth did not last two years and made only 33 appearances. Pearce stayed 12 seasons ("if they hadn't gone down again I would have been there for the rest of my career") and only Bob McKinlay (685) and Ian Bowyer (564) have played more games for the club.

In the early days his aggression could be brutal. Clough always liked his defenders to have a tough, streetwise edge and Ted McMinn and Pat Nevin are just two of the wingers who could testify for Pearce's ultra-competitive streak.

Neil Webb arrived at Forest in the same week as Pearce. "He was very quiet when I first met him," says Webb. "Extremely quiet, in fact. But his legs were massive - scarily so. He was never dirty but he was so strong and committed when he went for the ball he usually hurt his opponent as well. After his first year the word went round and right-wingers would not want to go anywhere near him."

As the game clamped down on robust tackling, Pearce had to modify his game accordingly but he retained his fearsome edge.

Michael Owen remembers one of his early games for Liverpool as Pearce walked past in the tunnel: "You're playing against me today, boy. Just you be careful."

Note the 'boy'. Owen recalls: "That day I thought: 'Oh Christ, this is serious - I'm a marked man now. This is what they warned me about'."

Pearce grins boyishly. "I had to change my style," he says. "The game changed so much over the years that by the end of my playing career giving away a foul was considered as bad a mistake as a misplaced pass.

"When I started out it was ridiculous what you could get away with. But in my defence the aggression I showed was always for a purpose rather than for the sake of stupidity.

"I remember playing for England against Yugoslavia and they had a guy who was running the show in midfield. So I didn't think it was a bad thing to scythe him down. I caught him late and it was a pretty bad tackle but there was a reason behind it. I knew if I could shake him up a bit he might not fancy it so much and they would go off the boil.

"Some people might not agree with that attitude but my disciplinary record bears out that I wasn't an idiot who would get booked and then carry on doing stupid things. I played more than 1,000 games and I was sent off only five times. One of those was for swearing and an average of one red card in every 200 matches isn't a great deal for someone with a so-called reputation."

It would be exaggerating to say Pearce did not bend the rules, but he was certainly not snide. You would never catch him stepping on an opponent's toes at a corner or scratching his nails down a rival's back. And he could take punishment as well as dish it out. In fact, you sensed he respected someone who had the courage to take him on. If anyone dumped him on the floor he would get up, dust himself down and get on with the match.

"Acknowledging pain was a form of weakness in my eyes," he says. If Pearce was hurt there was no way he would ever show it. Who else would have tried to run off a broken leg as he once did at West Ham?

The most notorious occasion occurred during England's game against France in the European Championships in 1992, when Basil Boli floored him with a flying headbutt in the midst of a congested penalty area. Pearce wore the line of blood under his eye like a fashion statement. Steaming mad, he promptly smashed a free-kick against Bruno Martini's crossbar but after the match he turned down every journalistic request to castigate Boli.

There were times when he found the 'Psycho' nickname faintly embarrassing (like when he was having dinner with his wife Liz and someone would shout it across the restaurant) but there is no doubt he lived up to the hard-man attitude.

"Brian Clough used to want all his players to show some form of moral courage - whether it was me standing up to people physically or Nigel taking the ball with his back to goal when Tony Adams and Steve Bould were crucifying him from behind.

"I've been in the tunnel when one of the opposition players has done something naughty. Cloughie would point his finger at him and growl: 'My captain will fucking have you.'

"That sort of thing used to give me a great sense of pride but I still say it was easier for me dishing it out than it was for Nigel. I never had anyone coming in behind me. He'd be standing there knowing he's going to take a bad one but still wanting the ball. That was real courage."

Pearce was the fourth Forest player after Tinsley Lindley, Frank Forman and Peter Shilton to captain England and he confounded those who suspected his formidable aggression would leave him exposed at the highest level.

It is largely overlooked, for example, that he had been arguably the outstanding left-back in Italia '90 and one of England's most impressive performers in the semi-final against Germany until *that* infamous penalty shoot-out miss.

Pearce is the kind of guy who would have the national anthem played at his wedding, a man more patriotic than a flag store. Along with Paul Gascoigne, he left Turin in tears. But how he reacted when he came back from Italy marked him down as a man of immense courage.

Even discounting his valour in stepping up to another penalty shoot-out to score against Spain in Euro '96 (when not even the most hard-nosed observer could fail to be swept along by the raw emotion) there was something wonderfully heroic about the way he used the most traumatic moment of his professional life as the catalyst for the best two years of his career.

Opposition fans would boo his every touch and treat him to choruses of "Pearce is a German" and "You let your country down" but it never flustered him. They tried it at Old Trafford and he silenced them with a terrific, swerving free-kick struck with such awesome power and accuracy the net billowed as though hit by a cannonball. In front of the Stretford End, too.

In 1990/91, he scored 16 goals (not one coming from the penalty spot) and was so imperious the Nottingham public demanded a steward's inquiry when Mark Hughes beat him to the Professional Footballers' Association player-of-the-year award and

Gordon Strachan did likewise for the Football Writers' Association trophy.

"It all came back to the have-a-go-at-me-and-it-will-make-me-stronger attitude," says Pearce. "I can't exaggerate how bad I felt after the World Cup. Missing that penalty was a huge blow in my life. Nowadays, it seems there's a penalty shoot-out drama in every tournament but it all felt new back then and the disappointment was excruciating.

"A lot of players might have gone under but my attitude has always been that you should use adversity to make you stronger. Seriously, the more people shouting abuse the better. It used to bring the best out of me.

"People often ask me about the most intimidating place I've ever played and I can honestly say there hasn't been anywhere. I would have the attitude: if the Man Utd fans are calling me a German they won't look so clever if I put a free-kick in the top corner.

"It came down to inner strength. Have you got it or not? I've been at Wembley before when John Barnes was being booed by our own fans. Even though he knew he was being hammered he still wanted the ball. So if he could do it so could I."

It is that attitude which ensures he has the respect of everyone in the game.

My favourite quote about Pearce comes from David Batty's autobiography: "I remember watching David Ginola and Lee Chapman file their nails in the dressing room and thinking: 'Bloody hell, what am I working with here?' They made me laugh, preening themselves like women getting ready on a night out. But Stuart Pearce was the complete opposite. He would come down to breakfast looking like he'd been dragged through a hedge, with hair all over the place. I appreciated that. He hadn't been poncing around in the bathroom for ages."

Batty goes on to describe his former England and Newcastle colleague as being "as good an example as I can think of for a successful, well-paid player who has never let wealth go to his head." It is a description Pearce must love. "I don't have a big ego and I always tried to give everything my best shot," he says. "I think that's what the Forest fans really liked. Hard work. They could look at me and see an ordinary fellow who would put everything into their club."

It is just a pity that by the end of Clough's final season their relationship had deteriorated to the point that a near-Trappist silence existed between them.

Clough says he lost respect for Pearce when he allegedly asked the club to double his £4,000 a week wages, despite still having three years of a five-year deal to run. Clough accused him of being "greedy" when he turned down a subsequent offer and was scathing of his former captain in his autobiography: "Stuart Pearce's heart no longer seemed to be in the club after he failed to get his way with the contract. He had a lot of trouble with injuries that season and there were times when we thought he was swinging the lead."

Clough's impression of Pearce was not helped when he aggravated a groin injury "doing somersaults" in training with England and, again, when one of his horses escaped from his stables in Langar and he tripped over some barbed wire trying to catch it.

Yet Pearce's version of events is quite different. He says Clough snubbed him by going on holiday to Cala Millor when they were supposed to be finalising the contract. According to him, the man whose opinion he valued above anyone then reneged on a second scheduled meeting. "I thought he let me down. He had his slant on things, I had mine - and we both thought we were right. But it's wrong to say we had a lot of ups and downs. That was the only time we really fell out and it happened in his last season.

"Apart from that we had a decent relationship. I had some great times with him and I will always be indebted to him for bringing me to the club and everything that he did for me.

"It wasn't just that he made me a better player, he made me a better man. He instilled the values of life into his players because he wanted them to be good people as well as good footballers. I'm eternally grateful for that. There were times, like when I came back from the World Cup in 1990 feeling desperately depressed, when he was there with an arm round my shoulder. He knew exactly what to do.

"It wasn't always easy. I remember the first time I was called up for the England squad and he called me into his office. I was expecting a pat on the back but I should have known better. 'I see you've been picked for England,' he said.

'Yes, boss.'

'Well, you aren't good enough in my opinion - now get out.'

"You'd walk out thinking: 'How dare you, you old bastard?' But if you had anything about you, you'd realise why he was doing it. He had different ways of knocking you down because he didn't want anybody to get above his station.

"There was psychology behind it. You would be desperate to show him that he was wrong and you would push the boundaries to prove you were good enough."

Pearce showed he had learned a thing or two in the wake of Frank Clark's departure when, filling in on a caretaker basis, Forest beat Arsenal in his first game ("I wrote out my team and then discovered I'd missed out a goalkeeper") and in January 1997 he became the first England international to win a manager-of-the-month award.

It was not enough, however, to prevent Forest sliding out of the Premiership (Pearce had taken over at a time when most of the damage had been done) and at the end of the season he decided it was time to sever his ties with the club, joining Newcastle on a free transfer. The *Nottingham Evening Post* responded by producing a 24-page supplement: 'Stuart Pearce: True Reds Hero.'

Gone but not forgotten, Pearce's popularity never diminished. The A-Block even started singing his name, demanding his instalment as manager, during those lamentable days under David Platt when the attendances dropped to their lowest mark for almost a quarter of a century.

If Clough could walk on water, Platt was a rusty old kettle at the bottom of the River Trent. Nobody shed any tears when he left to become the England under-21s' coach, but my view is that it would be a horrible shame if Pearce returned as manager and the adulation eroded in the face of a run of bad results - as happened, for example, with Billy Bonds at West Ham and Glenn Hoddle at Spurs.

# DEEP INTO THE FOREST

Typically, though, Pearce has never been one to walk away from a challenge. "Somewhere down the line I'd love to manage Forest. But in some ways, perhaps, I wonder sometimes if my popularity with the supporters might have held me back from getting the job.

"I've certainly applied for it before but there might be a mentality somewhere at the club that either I'm not good enough, not experienced enough or simply that they don't reckon it would work having me back. I'm not sure, really."

And his take on the supporters? "They were always loyal to me and I can never thank them enough. They were very patient at Forest. At West Ham, for example, their fans would let you know when things weren't quite right a lot quicker than they did in Nottingham.

"After the World Cup in 1990 I was feeling awful but the Forest fans were sensational. There were hundreds of letters of support - and none saying I'd let anybody down.

"It's a fantastic city. You could go out in the evening and people understood your privacy. In all the time I was there I can't think of one night when I had angry words with anyone. It was the ideal place to run my life and do something I loved doing.

"Even now most of the letters I get are from Forest fans. It's incredible, sometimes. I've walked out of the City Ground on many occasions and there would be people queuing up to say 'well done' when I knew deep down that I had played terribly. It didn't seem to matter even if I had had a shocker - they would still clap me off.

"Then there was the testimonial and there were so many people there that night they had to delay the kick-off by 15 minutes. You don't forget things like that. I remember in the build-up the feeling in and around Nottingham. It was a case of: whatever else you do, make sure you're there that night to say thank you to this fellow."

To put it into perspective, the testimonial match for Brian Clough and Peter Taylor against Derby in 1978 attracted a crowd of 18,000. Ian Bowyer's enticed around 7,000. Ditto Steve Sutton's. "It was a great honour," continues Pearce. "And it's because of that sort of thing why I say I could never play for Derby.

24

# STUART PEARCE

"It's not a throwaway remark. The point I'm trying to get across - and it's a valid one, no matter what some people might say - is that my relationship with Nottingham Forest and their supporters is too precious to me to jeopardise it by working for their local rivals.

"A lot of people will say I'm being short-sighted and that you can't make that sort of statement. But it will never come back to haunt me because that's the way I will always be. They would understand it in Nottingham, that's for sure, and they probably would in Derby, too. They might even wish some of their own players felt the same way about Forest."

Pearce's other great love, of course, is punk music and his face crumples with disgust when the subject turns to the watered-down tastes of his old teammates. This is a man who introduced the Sex Pistols on stage at Finsbury Park, who has been to see the Stranglers so many times they named a record label after him (Psycho Records) and whose pimply teenage mug can even be picked out on the front cover of a Lurkers album.

In Forest's run to the Uefa Cup quarter-finals in 1996 Pearce used to rouse his teammates by subjecting them to one of his Stiff Little Fingers albums, clenching his fists and screaming at the top of his voice: "Because we're English! Because we're English!" It did not seem to matter to him that sitting around him, trying not to look too conspicuously bemused, was a Dutchman, an Italian, a Norwegian, a Scot and a Welshman.

He laughs at the memory then turns serious. "They were great days but one of my biggest regrets is that we never had the chance to play in Europe more times," he says. "We didn't concede a goal in our first six matches on that Uefa Cup run. But I think we would have done even better under Brian Clough if it wasn't for the Heysel ban. His record in Europe was fantastic and our counter-attacking style would have been ideally suited to doing well.

"I always thought it was really unfair. Liverpool should have paid the price for what happened in the Heysel stadium rather than clubs like Forest who hadn't done anything wrong."

Assistant manager at Manchester City, he has been staying in a city-centre hotel, 200 miles from his picture-book thatched cottage in the Wiltshire countryside.

It cannot be easy, being so far from Liz and their two young children - Chelsea (despite being a boyhood QPR fan) and Harley Phoenix (named after the motorcycle and "cos if he's gonna be a rock star he's got to have a rock star's name"). But in many ways it is typical Pearce. He has always been willing to make sacrifices for his career and has never approached any part of his working life without the mentality that he has to put absolutely everything into it.

Nine years after aiming the ball too close to Bodo Illgner on July 4th, 1990, a letter dropped through his letterbox inviting him to Buckingham Palace to be made an MBE. As he says: "It was a world away from fixing toasters."

# Two

# Des Walker

*Des was an outstanding player and a world-class playboy.*

**Roy Keane**

DES WALKER IS NOT the only person in this book with a Top 40 song dedicated in his honour, but his is the only one to reach Number One. When KWS recorded their cover of KC & The Sunshine Band's 'Please Don't Go' in April 1992 it was in a bid to persuade Walker not to leave Forest. They even played a gig at the Black Orchid, Trentbeat's equivalent of the Cavern. But all to no avail. Walker left for Sampdoria, Forest were quickly relegated and KWS had to settle for 16 weeks on the chart and a nomination for Best New Act at the 1993 Brit Awards, alongside Undercover and the eventual winner, Tasmin 'voice of an era' Archer.

At least Walker had the decency to come back, although by then KWS had long since disbanded and, post-David Platt, Forest were in a state of convalescence. He played another two seasons and, even if we had seen his best days, it was worth it just to hear the schmaltzy cries of "You'll never beat Des Walker" floating across the City Ground once again. There were even calls for his No 4 jersey to be 'retired' when his creaking limbs finally told him it was time to call it a day and join the backroom staff at the grand old age of 38.

At his peak, Walker was class. Quietly efficient, totally unflappable and capable of doing 0-60mph before most sports cars had got into second gear, it would be impossible to recount all those times when an opposition striker had broken down the centre thinking he was clean through and, out of nowhere, Walker would effortlessly appear next to him and relieve him of possession with no fuss whatsoever.

# DEEP INTO THE FOREST

In two spells on Trentside he was a permanent fixture in the centre of defence for over a decade. Yet the strange thing is that even after more than 400 Forest appearances, a World Cup semi-final, 59 England caps (it should have been more), an FA Cup final own-goal and a spell in Serie A, he is still a closely guarded secret. Very little is known about Desmond Sinclair Walker.

Maybe that is not entirely surprising when you consider that until his second stint at the club Walker was famed for saying about as much in public as Chief Bromden in *One Flew Over the Cuckoo's Nest*. In two decades he has broken his self-imposed policy of *omertà* in a national newspaper on only two occasions. The first was with myself in the *Guardian*.

Did he enjoy the experience? Well, the *Observer* requested a follow-up interview and it took them five months to get a 'yes', and that was only after ambushing him in the City Ground car park one afternoon. Even then, Walker began with a word of warning for the journalist: "I don't want any Martin Bashir-type interview techniques."

To be granted an audience is something of a rarity then. It does not even matter that he is an hour late. A film crew from Sky is already at the City Ground and the man with the microphone is intrigued to find out Walker is on his way to the pressroom. "Ah, Des, he must be 57 this year . . ."

Not quite, but Walker acknowledges he "can hardly believe how quickly everything has happened" and there are times when he still refers to his playing days in the present tense, as if he is not quite accustomed to the fact he will never run out with the first-team again. "I'm enjoying the coaching," he says. "But the first thing it has taught me is that there is no better job in the world than being a player."

Walker arrived at Forest in 1983, a nervous 16-year-old from an estate in Hackney. He had been on schoolboy forms at Tottenham since the age of ten but for reasons known only to them they did not think the future England centre-half was worthy of a professional deal.

He nearly signed for Birmingham City and Aston Villa but was invited to the City Ground to play for the reserves, had a look round

# DES WALKER

Nottingham and preferred the vibes to Villa Park ("there was a kit-man who had something against Londoners") and St Andrews where Ron Saunders was the manager ("I wasn't signing for him").

"It was pretty daunting leaving my family and all my friends to head north and go to work for someone like Brian Clough," he says. "It was a big wrench. I wasn't even sure I wanted to leave London but as soon as I came to Forest it felt right. I look back now and it was the best decision I ever made."

Clough was in the process of building his second great Forest team. Not as good as the first one, admittedly. But a great team, nevertheless. In the nine seasons before Walker left for Italy Forest reached Wembley six times (one FA Cup final, three League Cups, one Simod Cup and one Zenith Data Systems Trophy) and never finished outside the top nine, including three top-three finishes. Had it not been for the Heysel ban they would have been in Europe almost every year.

"We were competing at the top end of the table and winning trophies at Wembley. It was a great time for the club with so many brilliant memories.

"People ask me what made that team special and the answer's simple: good players. When I joined there was Garry Birtles, Ian Bowyer, Paul Hart, Chris Fairclough, Steve Hodge, so there was a strong nucleus straight away. Then the club brought through the likes of Nigel Clough, and then Stuart Pearce and Neil Webb came in for small fees. They were all top players.

"The funny thing is that in my first four years we could never get past the third round in a cup competition but by the late-80s we were going back to Wembley every year. There was only Liverpool who were better than us in the country but there was a time when it felt as though Wembley was an annual part of the fixture list."

Walker is one of the few players whom Clough never castigated in public and the respect was mutual. "I consider myself lucky and privileged to have started my career under the greatest manager there has probably ever been. At that age he would let you know the fundamental basics of football and it would be embedded in you for the rest of your career.

# DEEP INTO THE FOREST

"I found him brilliant. Unpredictable, but brilliant. He always kept the game as simple as possible and he never asked you to do what you weren't good at. If you couldn't kick it with your right foot he would expect you to kick it with your left - but the thing is he would expect you to kick it well.

"If you could get used to his mannerisms you would be okay. Otherwise you would be in trouble. He would bark his orders at you and he never beat around the bush.

"I was under him for ten years and grew accustomed to the way he spoke to people so it wasn't a problem. He was a winner, I'm a winner - we both had that in common so it made sense that we got on."

Walker remembers Clough insisting the players reported for training the morning after they had beaten Luton in the 1989 League Cup final, Forest's first major trophy since the European Cup nine years earlier. It was a typical moment of Clough psychology - reminding everyone not to get carried away by their day in the sun.

"I thought: 'You can run me as hard you want - I've just won the final.'

"And he goes: 'We're going through the trees again because Desmond Walker didn't want to do it.'"

At times Clough's tongue could be brutal, even to a character as strong as Walker. Walker's mistakes are memorable simply because of their rarity but in the privacy of the dressing room there would still be periods when the sleek, athletic defender fell victim to his manager's tirades. Clough never let him forget the day, for example, when Tony Cottee scored a hat-trick against him at West Ham.

"He would let you know exactly what he thought of you and how you played," says Walker. "But I certainly wasn't frightened of him, like some people were. He expected me to do my job and I always thought that I could do that job, so I had nothing to fear."

Why Walker has always been so elusive is something of a mystery. Fleet Street had no choice but to grow accustomed to his silent, almost forbidding attitude. But when he went to Sampdoria the Italian press were never quite so forgiving. It did not reach the stage, as it did for Denis Law at Torino in 1961, where *Tuttosport* gave him their 'Premio Limone' award for being the player least inclined to co-operate with the press. But Walker's regulation 'no comment' certainly counted against him. He was heavily criticised for every small mistake and some of his most vociferous critics campaigned for Sven-Goran Eriksson, then Sampdoria's coach, to send him back to England at the earliest opportunity.

So what were his reasons? He is certainly not shy, or anything like it. Sat in his training kit, bouncing his legs up and down, Walker speaks 100-words-a-minute and it is difficult at times to keep up. When he used to room with Pearce for England matches his clubmate used to complain that he could hardly get a word in edgeways.

Nor is he short of personality. Have a Saturday night out in the Lace Market and you would be odds on to bump into Walker in one of the Nottingham glitterati's favourite nightspots. There are stories (probably best not repeated within earshot of Forest's insurers) of him being obsessed with high-powered motorcycles and doing 120mph wheelies on disused airfields. And Roy Keane speaks of a social animal "who owned the cars, wore the clothes and pulled the girls - he liked a drink and he was great company after dark."

Had Walker been a bit more open with the press he might have found that having a few friends in Fleet Street would benefit him at various stages of his career - but he does not have any regrets.

"I always saw myself as a footballer and nothing else. I wasn't a broadcaster or a writer. I never came to this club and said I wanted to be a journalist. And I never wanted to see myself talking on television or in the newspapers.

"I considered myself as being good at football rather than public speaking. I would watch Gary Lineker and David Platt and think, okay, they're good at it. Then, at the other end of the scale would be Gazza, who was no good at it whatsoever but couldn't help himself.

"You have to be true to yourself and I made my choice at an early age. There are lot of people in this game who never seem to be off the television and, for some reason, they think it's natural. But I could never see it that way. I'm an individual, not a sheep."

# DEEP INTO THE FOREST

As well as being a reluctant interviewee, Walker was a less-than-enthusiastic goalscorer. In 21 years his return was one - a last-minute equaliser against Luton (with Steve Sutton, on loan from Forest, in the opposing goal) on a freezing New Year's Day in 1992.

The irony was that Clough actually missed it because Forest had been so dismal he was already on his way down the tunnel to wait in the dressing room for his players. Whether Walker spared his teammates the snakelick of Clough's tongue is unclear but it is certainly true that for 89 minutes the crowd had been subjected to one of the worst displays of the season.

What followed was a reward for anyone who had resisted the temptation to head off a few minutes early. So rare were Walker's forays the other side of the halfway line the old line went that he used to get a nosebleed if he went that high up the pitch. So it almost felt like a trick of the imagination when he collected the ball inside his own half, burst forward and, gulp, continued running. A lovely pass from Nigel Clough and suddenly he was inside the penalty area. Then the ball was in the back of the net and Walker was haring back to his own goal like Forrest Gump on amphetamines. Strange how a 1-1 draw against Luton can be so memorable.

"It was a bit of a mental celebration. Yeah, a good moment." He pauses. "I wouldn't describe it as one of my high points, though. The high points for me were defending well 50 times a season. In my role, a clean sheet was much more of a buzz. I was happy to leave scoring to the strikers."

It was the following summer that Walker ignored KWS's heartfelt plea and joined the likes of Roberto Mancini and Attilio Lombardo at Sampdoria, exploiting a clause in his contract that stipulated he could leave if a foreign club made a bid of £1.5m, less than half his true worth.

"We've lost the battle - Walker on his way," groaned the headline in the *Nottingham Evening Post*.

It was a transfer that can be brought out as Exhibit A in explaining the club's relegation the following season. Suddenly there was no Walker to mind the shop and cover for the other defenders with his supreme pace. Stuart Pearce had to redefine himself as a more orthodox full-back and cut back on his forward surges, meaning Forest suffered in attack too. Clough had brought in Carl Tiler the previous season and he stepped into Walker's role, which was a bit like trading in a Jaguar for a Vauxhall Astra.

"It was a hard decision to leave. Because I'd been at Forest so long it was always going to be an emotional wrench," explains Walker. "Unfortunately I didn't think the club were moving forwards in terms of buying players.

"We were still in Liverpool's shade and I wanted a new challenge. Playing for England had put me up against some of the best strikers in the world and I wanted that sort of challenge every week. All the top forwards seemed to play in Serie A so Italy was the logical choice. But it still hurt seeing the club drop out of the top division. I might not have been there but I knew how everyone would be feeling."

Walker's Italian career actually began with a match against Forest in the Makita tournament in Leeds and he played in 30 out of a possible 34 games for Sampdoria, the defeated European Cup finalists. Yet it was not quite the experience he expected or wanted, largely due to Eriksson's bewildering insistence on playing him at left-back.

Walker's discomfort was obvious. He was back in the Premiership with Sheffield Wednesday after just one season but near-irreparable damage had been inflicted on his reputation as England's premier defender, culminating with him all but disappearing from the international scene after giving away a penalty three minutes before the end of a World Cup qualifier against Holland.

England had been leading by two goals and were coasting before Holland came back into the game and pulled a goal back. Walker then allowed Marc Overmars to sprint past him and, desperate to make amends, brought him down as he tore into the penalty area.

Seeing him being outpaced was an exceptional moment and he was vilified in the media. Maybe partly due to his unwillingness ever to speak to Fleet Street's finest (journalists used to adapt the famous chant to "we'll never meet Des Walker") the list of sports writers willing to pen anything in his defence could have been scribbled on the back of a postage stamp. Holland equalised and the upshot was that Walker found himself written-off at the age of 27.

Too much has happened since then for someone of his secretive nature to be openly bitter, but he is entitled to harbour some private grievances. It is unlikely, for instance, that he has too many good things to say about Graham Taylor.

It is difficult not to feel he was hard done by. If Walker had played for a more fashionable team he would surely have made his England debut long before Bobby Robson (under pressure from Clough) finally saw the light and brought him into his side to face Norway in 1988. And in terms of consistency it is difficult to remember another defender, at Forest or anywhere else, who could compare favourably. Or, indeed, anyone who was as clean and precise in the tackle.

Seasoned internationals usually have one characteristic that distinguishes them from other players and Walker's was not just his ability to cruise past opponents with one of those searing bursts of acceleration but his reading of the game and his ability to sense danger. His exemplary sense of timing made it a rarity for referees even to have to speak to him, let alone consider taking out their notebook. And it was largely due to Walker's supreme covering skills that Pearce had carte blanche to go forward so many times, knowing full well that if the play suddenly changed direction his teammate would almost inevitably get him out of trouble.

Walker was anything but error-prone but it was his misfortune that the few mistakes he made came in high-profile matches. His England career all but disintegrated in the time it took for Overmars to sprint past him and go down under his challenge at Wembley. His second spell at Forest included the heartache of an own-goal in the second leg of the First Division play-off semi-final against Sheffield United. And then, of course, there was the 1991 FA Cup final.

How unfair that Walker will be forever associated for his unwitting contribution to Forest's 2-1 defeat to Tottenham when the majority of blame should really be laid at the door of the referee Roger Milford. In the history of villainous FA Cup moments it is impossible to find anything remotely comparable to the fouls (if that is the right word) that Paul Gascoigne perpetrated on Garry Parker and Gary Charles at Wembley. Had Milford done his job correctly and sent off Gascoigne the numerical advantage would surely have worked in Forest's favour, especially after Pearce had rammed one of his trademark free-kicks into the top corner of the Spurs net. Instead, Spurs gradually clawed their way back into the match, equalised through Paul Stewart and took it into extra time.

The rest is history that Walker would rather not dwell upon. Nayim took a corner from the right, Stewart flicked it on and Gary Mabbutt, an FA Cup loser in 1987 because of his own-goal against Coventry, came charging in at the far post.

"All I remember is that I had to get there," says Walker. "It was like slow motion, I headed the ball and as I was landing I was thinking: 'Oh no, it's going in . . .'

"The most depressing thing for me was that there were 30,000 Forest fans who had made the journey down from Nottingham. They were all behind that bloody goal and as the ball went in it just went quiet. It must have been such a downer for them.

"I'm never going to get a chance to put it right and people will always ask me about it. But regrets? I'm not sure about that. Obviously I regret the fact it went in and we lost the game because of it. But I can't regret my decision to go for the ball because that's what I had to do.

"I just had to remind myself as quickly as possible that going for those sort of balls was what I was paid to do. You get those moments of bad luck but as long as you know in your own mind you were doing the right thing you have to carry on."

Did it affect his confidence? "Not at all. I was always going to recover quickly because we had a match the following week (England went on tour to Australia and New Zealand) so I had to refocus. It would have been no good playing for the rest of my career worrying about an own-goal. So it went out of my head as soon as I played my next match. And my conscience was clear.

# DEEP INTO THE FOREST

"I was a professional footballer and my job was to try to head the ball clear. I could have stood there and watched their player head it in or, as I did, I could have tried to get in front of him and head it clear. So what do you do? If the same cross came over 5,000 times, I would always try to get there first."

Walker's philosophical outlook should not be misconstrued as a lack of feeling. The images of May 18th, 1991, tell another story. As Mabbutt lifted the trophy Walker was lying flat out on the turf, picking out pieces of grass and lost in his own thoughts. The pain had been etched on his features as he collected his loser's medal and there was nothing anybody could say to console him in the dressing room.

Whereas Walker had comforted Pearce after his penalty shoot-out miss in the World Cup semi-final against Germany ten months earlier, this time the roles were reversed. Pearce has always been grateful for the way Walker helped him get over the most harrowing moment of his career. On this occasion Pearce remembers his friend being "distraught, absolutely gutted."

"The fans were brilliant as well," says Walker. "I must have had thousands of letters. That meant a lot to me because it had been the biggest game involving the club for a long, long time.

"Everyone let me know that they were thinking of me, that they appreciated me and that nobody blamed me. It was great because no footballer wants to be judged by one second of their career, especially when they have been at the same club for nearly ten years. The supporters let me know that wasn't the case and I really appreciated that."

His route back to Forest was anything but straightforward. Walker performed under eight different managers at Wednesday, made more than 350 appearances and was the fans' player-of-the-year in the 1993/94 season. But when they could not afford to renew his contract he found himself a victim of the spiralling finances outside the top division.

He had one game for Nigel Clough's Burton Albion then decided to try his luck in America. He played for the New York Metro Stars in their September 11th benefit matches against DC United. Then an offer was made to take a coaching role in Major League Soccer.

# DES WALKER

At first the idea appealed but when the time arrived his children, Tiler and Lewis, were starting school and he could not go through with it. "I didn't want to drag them with me and I just asked myself whether I wanted to be away from them for six months."

Unfit and unwanted, it was only when he asked Paul Hart if he could train with Forest that the opportunity arose to resurrect a career that had been gathering dust for the previous 15 months.

Hart had played alongside the teenage Walker when he made his debut as a right-back in a 1-0 defeat of Everton in March 1984. He was impressed by Walker's dedication, urged him to get fit and offered him a contract and the club captaincy.

"I had to do a lot of hard thinking," says Walker. "I could have tried America but it would have been too much of a wrench being apart from my sons. Or I could have retired there and then. I was 36 and I'd had a good run.

"The one thing I always knew was that if I was going to start playing again it had to feel right. I didn't want to play for a manager I didn't see eye to eye with. Then Forest came along and Paul Hart was someone I always respected. They were the right club at the right time. They were looking for an experienced defender and I fitted the bill.

"Because of Paul's work with the youth academy there were the likes of Gareth Williams, Michael Dawson and Jermaine Jenas. It was the best group of young players I've ever seen together under one roof.

"The only problem was that I hadn't played for nine months. I was a bit unsure at first so I asked if I could get myself fit first and then see how I felt. As it turned out, I felt pretty good. I got another two years out of it and, for that, I will always be grateful."

He returned to a club ravaged by financial difficulties, ensconced in the middle reaches of the First Division and struggling to recuperate from David Platt's bewildering spell as manager. Yet in Walker's first season they defied all expectations to reach the play-offs, with him and Dawson (18 years his junior) the lynchpins in defence.

The anguish that accompanied his own-goal against Sheffield United was compounded by the fact he had been Forest's outstanding player on a night when so many of his teammates had been affected by nerves. But, again, the sackloads of supportive mail helped ease the pain.

"The fans have always been great with me," he concludes. "I'd like to think they appreciated the effort and the commitment I put in - much like they did with Pearcey."

It has become apparent, however, that he is not the nostalgic type. "It's easy sometimes to talk about what has gone before rather than what's going to happen. You can't keep harping back to the past. There aren't that many Roy Keanes in a generation. There aren't that many Stuart Pearces, Nigel Cloughs, Archie Gemmills, Trevor Francises. In 25 years we have had some great players but it's no use moaning that we haven't anyone like that now."

And then he is up and gone before there is even time to wish him good luck. It is difficult to know what to make of him. Very difficult. Maybe it was just unfortunate to pick a day when, taking training, he had landed awkwardly on the hand he broke at West Bromwich Albion in the final game of the 2003/04 season. Walker was in such discomfort he could not even shake hands and there were moments when he was not an enthusiastic interviewee, to say the least. For example. . ."What about your policy of not speaking to the press?"

"There was no policy." Or . . .

"You've always had a great affinity with the fans, Des."

"I wouldn't say that - they don't have their favourites." Oh, really?

It is easy to understand why David Pleat, one of his former managers at Sheffield Wednesday, once remarked: "Much as I would have liked to, I always found it hard to communicate with him."

No big deal. Walker was undoubtedly the outstanding England defender of his generation and, all in all, it does not really matter if he would rather shy away from publicity.

One game, in particular, stands out. Forest were playing Tottenham, the club that had rejected him as a teenager, and he was meant to be at home with a virus. He played, kept Gary Lineker in his pocket and afterwards Clough claimed he would have started with Walker even if it had meant bringing him out on his sickbed.

After everything he had done for Forest it was only right that Joe Kinnear invited him to join the backroom staff as a mentor for the younger players and it will be a sad day when he finally severs his ties with the club.

So one last time, Des . . .

*I love you*
*Yeah*
*Babe, I love you so*
*I want you to know*
*That I'm going to miss your love*
*The minute you walk out that door*
*So please don't go. Don't go*
*Don't go away*
*Please don't go*
*Don't go*
*I'm begging you to stay*
*If you leave*
*At least in my lifetime*
*I've had one dream come true*
*I was blessed to be loved*
*By someone as wonderful as you*
*So please don't go*
*Don't go.*

# THREE

# Trevor Francis

*When I sit in my garden and close my eyes I can
still see that moment in Munich. Trevor Francis is hurtling
towards the far post, and Robbo sends in the perfect cross.
One-nil. Pass me the European Cup. Thank you.*

**Brian Clough.**

TREVOR FRANCIS IS stirring a café latte and reliving the day the
blood in his veins felt as though it had been converted to red wine.
The date was May 30th, 1979, the venue was Munich's Olympic
stadium and the occasion was the European Cup final. Francis has
just headed in the winning goal ("the best feeling I've ever
experienced") and 30,000 travelling fans are in the vortex of the
greatest moment of their lives. It is an orgy of screaming, dribbling,
screaming, jumping, screaming, hugging, crying and more
screaming. Oktoberfest must have felt tame by comparison.
Munich might be famous for its beer festival but there is nothing
like being drunk on the taste of euphoria.

How do you begin to sum up the emotions of that night? For
Brian Clough it was the zenith of his work at a club he had found
wallowing in apathy four years earlier. For the directors it was the
reward for hiring a man whose contract presumably included the
small print that he would seldom treat them with anything but
contempt. For the supporters it was the moment all that pent-up
longing and all those years of unfulfilled dreams and yearning for
success reached a glorious climax. And for Francis it was, in his
words, "the stuff dreams are made of."

The man who will forever be known at the City Ground as 'Sir
Trev' should never have to put his hand in his pocket in a
Nottingham pub for the rest of his life. Yet every time he speaks of

that magical night (and it says much about his modest nature that he does so only when asked) he begins by recognising how different it might have been.

"If things had worked out less fortunately I might have spent the entire night on the bench," he says. "I'd cost Forest £1m, making me the most expensive footballer in history, but had never been involved in a European match and it rested entirely on whether Brian Clough reckoned Martin O'Neill and Archie Gemmill were fit. I really do consider myself very, very lucky.

"We had taken a bus to the stadium in the morning, had a walk on the pitch, then sat on the perimeter track and Clough went round each of us telling us who was playing and who was not. You could have heard a pin drop. For me, it was a massive relief and it was difficult not to show that. But I also wanted to be dignified because I knew people were sat by me suffering. I'll always remember how desperately disappointed Martin and Archie were. I never actually looked in their eyes but I didn't have to. None of us did."

Francis never seems happier than when he is reminiscing about Forest's 1-0 defeat of Malmo and it soon becomes apparent he remembers virtually every moment, from the coach ride to the stadium and the nerves in the tunnel to the first reassuring touch of the ball and the rush of euphoria as he realised the glory was his.

Clough had always preached that a player's first touch set the standard for his performance but some of his most reliable first-teamers seemed to have frozen under the burden of being such overwhelming favourites. Kenny Burns, for example, began with a nervous header back to Peter Shilton that landed on the foot of a Malmo striker, Jan Olav Kindrall, who was taken by surprise and too slow to react. But Francis played with such carefree abandon it was as if he was immune to fear. His was the most assured touch, the most graceful movement and the most positive thinking. He was the outstanding player bar none.

"The goal still has a dreamlike quality," he says. "I was playing on the right of midfield and it was always drummed into me that when the ball was on the left, and particularly when John Robertson was in possession, it was my responsibility to get to that far post.

"I had 40 yards to make up but I timed my run to perfection. The cross went over the goalkeeper and I just had to get behind the ball and direct it back towards the net. I knew that if I could make a good contact there was only one place the ball would end up. And then it was in and I was hitting the floor and up celebrating the greatest moment of my life."

Francis landed on the shot-putters' circle behind the pitch. "The funny thing is I get asked about that more than the goal but, even if it looked concrete, the truth is it was actually rubber. I wasn't as brave as people imagine although I was on such a high at that point I'd have felt fine even if it was concrete."

His outstanding memory is of the raucous celebrations, of scarcely being able to sleep and of the mother of all homecomings. An estimated 200,000 fans had converged on Nottingham to see the team parade the trophy from an open-top bus. They had taken up their positions up to nine hours before it even set off - scaling lampposts, balconies, spires and anywhere else where it was possible to get a good view. "It was like a ribbon of red," says Francis. "As the bus inched towards the city centre they did not so much line the route as engulf it. That sort of thing lasts with you forever."

At the 25th anniversary reunion dinner Francis was sat on the top table as the highlights were shown on a giant screen. As he stretches to head in Robertson's cross, Barry Davies's television commentary kicks in:

*Well, that's what I wanted to see Robertson do. And Trevor Francis, the million pounds man, puts his name on the score-sheet and returns a great deal of the cheque.*

Robertson was actually irritated by the perceived slight ("it's all well and good saying that, but defenders don't just allow you to do what you want - they weren't idiots") but Francis loves that commentary, particularly the bit about repaying his price tag.

"I didn't like to admit it back then but I have to admit there were times when I found the million-pound label suffocating," he says. "I never thought it would bother me as much as it did but, if I'm being totally honest, it was a massive relief when Steve Daley was transferred for £1.4m and the pressure was taken off me.

# TREVOR FRANCIS

"Until then everyone had focused on me. My first full match for Forest was at Ipswich and the abuse was merciless. I tried to blank it out when the match was in progress but it was impossible when there were stoppages. Every time the game stopped all I could hear was 'What a waste of money' going round the ground, over and over again.

"It was a tough day and it did get to me. I was so keen to do well and I was desperate for a goal. In the end I resorted to cheating. A cross came in that was just a few centimetres too high and when I realised I wasn't going to reach it with my head I punched the ball in the back of the net. I didn't get away with it with the referee and, even worse, I didn't get away with it in the dressing room.

"Clough let me know in no uncertain terms what he thought of me: 'If you're going to play in my team we don't want any of that crap. We play by the rules here and I don't want to see that ever again.' That was my first major bollocking and getting bawled out by Clough was not a pleasant experience. I've had better days, put it that way."

A Larry Lloyd-esque weight lifted from his shoulders when, 28 days later, he registered his first goal for the club, a last-minute equaliser in a 1-1 home draw against Bolton.

"It was such a relief. Being the first £1m footballer was hard enough but there was also the fact that playing for Brian Clough made it so much more difficult in terms of pressure.

"You have to remember he was an outstanding forward in his own right and because of that he set extremely high standards for his strikers. According to him any sort of chance around the penalty area was a good chance. So a lot was expected from him and even more from the media.

"In those early days my mistake was trying to justify being a £1m footballer in every second of every match. Eventually I realised I would be much better off performing like the player that had scored all those goals at Birmingham.

"Once that happened I never felt the same pressure and overall I'd say I had a good relationship with Clough. His memorial service could have been anywhere in the world and I would have been there.

# DEEP INTO THE FOREST

"I know a lot of people think he ruled by fear, but I don't go along with that theory. Okay, he left you in absolutely no doubt he was the boss. He could be extremely cutting and a strict disciplinarian but if everyone was frightened of him how come the players were able to perform as they did? If he ruled by fear there would have been too much tension for the players to express themselves.

"A better way to put it is that he had a unique ability to be constantly on top of his players, even bullying them sometimes, but when you left that dressing room at five to three he had managed to leave everyone feeling totally relaxed. He was eccentric at times, but he was also incredibly intelligent and nothing ever escaped him - you couldn't get away with anything.

"The best example I can give is that on those occasions when you had to run that extra two or three yards, maybe to charge down a clearance or put the ball out for a throw-in, there are some players who might think twice about it and hope that it won't really be noticed. Not at Forest. With Brian Clough around, you never thought twice. Because you knew that if you didn't [he snaps his fingers] he would be on top of you straight away. And he would think nothing of humiliating you in that dressing room.

"We had poor old Frank Gray who was a very good attacking left-back. Getting forward was definitely his strength but he wasn't the most outstanding natural defender, so a typical quote at half-time would be Clough shouting: 'Frank, you aren't getting forward enough, get in their box otherwise get off that pitch and in the bath.'

"What he was effectively telling everyone was: 'Frank, do what you're good at because defensively you aren't good enough.' It could be merciless at times. That tongue could destroy you when he got going and Peter Taylor was just as cutting when he wanted."

Even in the warm afterglow of Munich Francis was not spared their caustic observations. As if it were not bad enough that on the plane home Taylor described him to journalists as "a disgrace to his profession at Birmingham," Clough went on television to claim Francis had "won a medal by fluke".

Francis won 52 England caps under three different managers and could turn a game with a pass, a run or a goal. Yet Clough used to complain that his most expensive recruit lacked the devilish instincts and aggression that set a forward such as Denis Law apart.

Even when Francis was taking his first, tentative steps into management Clough could not resist the opportunity to write him off as being "too nice" to be successful. It was probably with this in mind that Francis subsequently dropped Martin Allen from his plans at QPR because he had missed a match to be at the birth of his first child (Francis later apologised). Even more infamously, his time as Crystal Palace manager was memorable for all the wrong reasons after he "cuffed" his substitute goalkeeper Alex Kolinko, whom he suspected of laughing when they conceded an early goal to Bradford City. "Clough was a one-off," he says, shaking his head. "There was no point in anyone trying to copy him."

Their first meeting was a classic: in 1977 Clough was due to present Francis with the ATV Midlands player-of-the-year award and, live on television, chastised him for having his hands in his pocket. Clough delivered the line like a Victorian schoolmaster. "Yes sir," Francis replied meekly, as if to illustrate the point.

"I wasn't too impressed," says Francis. "But he could be equally as kind. Totally unannounced, you might find that he had sent your wife a bunch of red roses or a lovely piece of porcelain. He was absolutely charming when he wanted to be.

"He had a great way of sweet-talking people although, if I'm being honest, I didn't really need him to sell Forest to me. My reason for wanting to leave Birmingham was that I had played for long enough in a team languishing towards the lower reaches of the league. I wanted to play in a winning team and get some medals and, quite simply, I felt Forest gave me a much better chance of doing that than anyone else.

"There were other clubs interested and Coventry had made me an offer that was probably superior in financial terms to the one at Forest. But when I heard Forest had matched Birmingham's valuation I'd set my heart on it before we even started talking.

"Birmingham had made it clear they wouldn't accept a penny less than £1m but I have to say I didn't realise at the time how significant it was. It's only as the years have passed me by that I have started realising what it meant to be known as 'the first £1m footballer.'

"That's still how I get introduced at social functions. And I get dads coming up to me with their children telling them about it. You can see these kids of seven and eight looking up at me, clearly not having a clue who I am, and thinking: 'well that's nothing!' These days it's not much more impressive than a free transfer."

The history-making moment went though on February 8th, 1979, but not before a prolonged period of haggling between the two clubs and some frenzied media speculation about how Kenny Burns would react to the news.

"Kenny and myself didn't always see eye to eye at Birmingham," explains Francis. "Some people felt it might even prevent me from going to Forest, but it would have been totally wrong for me to allow something like that to influence such a major career decision.

"I had to be professional. Kenny was one of the first players I saw when I came to Nottingham to train for the first time. Jimmy Gordon introduced me to everyone and I shook hands with them all, including Kenny."

Personality clashes are hardly to be unexpected in the unnatural surroundings of a dressing room when players from vastly differing backgrounds and upbringings are lumped together and required to be friends. Francis believed a player had "failed" if he was booked, something that happened to him only twice during his career. Burns, in stark contrast, was the Glaswegian hard-man who, in Mark Lawrenson's words, would "try to assassinate the centre-forward in the first 30 minutes." Burns has subsequently put the friction down to envy and immaturity on his part, not least because Francis "was driving a TR6 while I had an Austin 1100".

He resented the fact that Francis "had everything so young" and came from a demonstrably loving home. In the early days Francis's father Roy, a shift foreman for the South West Gas Board, would think nothing of making the seven-hour journey to St Andrew's from Plymouth (before the days of the M5) while the player's mother Phyllis would raise petrol money by doing sewing and tailoring locally at six shillings an hour.

# TREVOR FRANCIS

Even while playing as dual strikers at St Andrew's, Francis and Burns could go an entire game without sharing a single word. The mutual antipathy manifested itself in training one day when Francis was so appalled by an industrial challenge from his supposed 'teammate' that he stomped off Birmingham's training ground and three days later submitted a transfer request, even though he claimed it was unrelated.

"A lot of stuff was written about Kenny and myself but I have to say that it was widely exaggerated," says Francis. "It was quickly sorted and we used to laugh about it afterwards. When I joined Forest, the way he conducted himself and his approach to the game, he was unrecognisable from the Kenny Burns at Birmingham. Brian Clough had completely changed him."

In his first season the suspicion was that Clough and Taylor were harder on Francis than any other player, a theory that gathered pace when they made him make his debut in the Midlands Intermediate League against Notts County on a frozen pitch on the banks of the Trent.

Francis says there was a much more simple explanation. "People ask me whether I found playing in the A-team demeaning and a lot was made of it at the time because it was seen as a classic example of Clough immediately putting me down and reminding everyone who was boss.

"Everyone construed it as a message that however much I cost he still had the power to stick me in the third team. But I didn't take it like that and I'm convinced it wasn't meant as an insult.

"The fact is that it had been an extremely cold period when a lot of first-team games were being called off. I'd been inactive anyway because of an injury so it was a good opportunity to get some match practice on an available pitch."

Hardly erasing the suspicion that a record transfer fee might see him temporarily forget his humble upbringing on a Plymouth council estate, Francis drove up to the pitch in his Jaguar. But he failed to score in a 2-2 draw and it was an inauspicious start, especially when Forest were fined £250 under a Football League charge of playing him in a match when his transfer was still not registered.

# DEEP INTO THE FOREST

"It wasn't quite two men and a dog, but there were no more than 30 people there. My abiding memory is of Clough giving me a lecture at half-time because I wasn't wearing shin pads. It wasn't a mandatory rule in those days and I didn't like wearing them. But he made it clear that if I wanted to last longer than one match I had to change my ways. So I had to find someone to lend me some pads for the second half.

"Apart from that there was one moment when I missed a shot and a fellow on the sideline shouted: 'You'll have to do better than that, Francis.' Clough ran almost halfway round the pitch to confront him. 'His name's *Trevor*'."

Fast-forward a quarter of a century and Francis would make a drab feature on the BBC's *Through The Keyhole*. Visitors to the Francis household in Dorridge, one of Birmingham's swankier suburbs, might even struggle to work out this is the home of a former footballer. True, the videos of Forest's European excursions offer one clue, but the place is conspicuously lacking photographs of those heady nights. There are no shots of him landing on the shot-putters' circle in Munich, no England shirts framed on the wall and none of the trophy cabinets that most footballers consider mandatory to show-off their prized possessions.

"I'm not a showy person," he explains. And his European Cup winner's medal? "Sorry, it's in the vault of a bank. If you're asking to see it - as my sons often do - I'll have to apologise because I can't do it. I pay a set amount each year to keep it safe. I just treasure it too much to take any risks. You read about players whose medals have been stolen and it must be heartbreaking. And not many footballers are lucky enough to get a European Cup winners' medal."

It can feel like a trick of the mind that there was once a time when he was afforded the type of superstar status to which no footballer apart from Kevin Keegan had ever been exposed.

Francis's every move was scrutinised by the media and, in turn, he found himself inundated with marketing offers. Adidas made him their first contracted footballer in England, having concentrated until then on German stars such as Franz Beckenbauer, Gerd Muller, Uwe Seeler and Klaus Fischer.

# TREVOR FRANCIS

Even *Woman's Own* jumped on the bandwagon, running a feature about how Francis had met his wife Helen on holiday - a romantic mini-novel in which he lost her telephone number, could remember only that she worked as a hairdresser in Llanelli and systematically began ringing every salon in the telephone book until he located her on the fifteenth call.

But there was a downside too. A begging letter arrived from a woman claiming her husband had been sacked from his job. Would Trevor be kind enough to send them a cheque so they could afford to go out for dinner on their wedding anniversary? Others quickly followed, including one from a man asking for £5,000 so he could give up his job and concentrate on his love for writing poetry.

When Francis was house-hunting in Nottingham he suspected the prices were being hiked simply because it was him, and he still remembers the anger of his father-in-law when a passer-by piped up: "New suit? I take it Trevor bought you that."

Francis was entitled to a standard five per cent cut of the transfer fee, earning him £50,000, but it was often overlooked that by leaving Birmingham he had turned his back on a testimonial that would have rewarded him with possibly twice that amount.

The simple fact was that he had outgrown the West Midlands club. Francis had scored 15 goals in his first 15 matches (including four one day against Bolton) before he had reached his 17th birthday. He was dubbed 'Super Boy' by the brilliantly imaginative media (he had scored 800 goals in Devon schools football) and his impact during those early days could be gauged by the headlines on the BBC's *Sports Report* one night: "And Trevor Francis did not score today!"

Birmingham, however, were bottom of the league when he left and his talents clearly deserved a higher stage. Francis had become the hottest property in English football with journalists hanging on his every move.

"At 16 I was making headlines on the front pages as well the back pages," Francis says of the press publicity. "Media-wise, it was a case of sink or swim very early in my career.

"It could be a problem sometimes but it came in useful when I went to Forest. I was always able to handle the media attention. It was still strange seeing myself on the nine o'clock news but the press never really fazed me.

"I just had to learn that being the first £1m footballer gave me a profile that meant if there was anything of remote interest that could be written about me, you could be certain it would appear in print. It didn't seem to matter how insignificant it was. They had a field day, for example, when they found out Clough had told me to make the tea for everyone one day.

"I couldn't believe the press swallowed Clough's tongue-in-cheek remarks. All the newspapers started calling me the '£1m Teaboy' but, again, Clough hadn't meant it to be demeaning. I had signed too late to play in the League Cup or the rounds of the European Cup before the final but I used to travel with the squad anyway, and Clough's mentality was that everyone had to do something, no matter how menial, if it helped the starting XI get the result.

"After one game he turned to me: 'Trev, put the kettle on for your mates, they've just earned you a win bonus.' Other times you might have to collect the shirts. It was the same for Peter Shilton, John Robertson and everybody and I didn't mind one bit."

Even now it takes some believing that Francis had been at the club only 111 days and played just 20 matches when he won the European Cup. His far-post header was his sixth goal for the club and it was not until the following season that he truly established himself as the most lethal finisher in the country, averaging a goal every other game before his dreams of a second European Cup medal took on nightmarish proportions.

Football can be brutally cruel sometimes and Francis must have wondered what he had ever done to deserve the misery that accompanied rupturing his Achilles tendon against Crystal Palace in the penultimate home match of the 1979/80 season - only 25 days before the European Cup final against Hamburg.

Even now he winces at the memory. "There might have been questions about the rights and wrongs of selecting me for the first final, but there certainly wouldn't have been for that second one.

"I did as much as anyone to get us into that final so it was just Sod's law. It was the second-last game of the season, we were four up against Crystal Palace, I'd got two of them and I was looking for a hat-trick with ten minutes to go.

"There was absolutely no warning but the pain was so excruciating I've never experienced anything quite like it before. My first thought - and I mean this - was that someone in the crowd must have shot me. I was just lying there in absolute agony and when I was carted off to hospital they told me I would be out for seven or eight months. Not only did it mean I missed out on the European Cup final but it also ruled me out of the European Championship with England.

"If the first final ranks as the highlight of my career, that injury has to be the low point. I was so looking forward to that final but I wasn't even allowed to travel with the squad.

"To put it bluntly, Cloughie didn't want me there. Out of the blue one day I had a phone call from his secretary informing me that I had to stay away. He didn't like injured players cluttering up the place and he felt that, psychologically, me turning up on crutches would have a bad effect on the team.

"I wouldn't have moped around but I had no choice. So I went on holiday to the south of France and watched the match in the television room of my hotel in Cannes. To describe it as surreal would be an understatement. There were so many different emotions going on in my head.

"On one hand I was absolutely delighted, on the other I was totally devastated. Every footballer has ups and downs in their career but in the course of two seasons not many could have lurched between the highs and lows I went through."

Francis worked manically to regain his fitness but one disappointment followed another within eight months of completing his rehabilitation. Criticising Clough's decision-making always seems such an act of folly, like taking Tiger Woods to task over his backswing or quibbling about the way Michael Schumacher changes gear. But replacing Francis with Justin Fashanu was like asking a painter and decorator to do the job of a landscape artist.

Francis had not even completed a century of matches for the club when he was informed, against his wishes, that he was being sold to Manchester City. Forest had already turned down two bids from Barcelona but the transfer to Maine Road was completed with obscene hastiness. Forest recouped their £1m but, quite simply, were never the same again.

"I've never been given an explanation. What I will say, though, is that I did not want to leave. At the time nothing was ever said but I'd like to make it clear that I was very happy at Forest. I'd made a complete recovery from the Achilles injury, played numerous games and proved that I was every bit as good, if not better, than before.

"But it became apparent that summer that something might be going on behind the scenes. I'll always remember sitting at Trent Bridge watching the cricket and seeing a copy of the *Nottingham Evening Post* saying that Peter Shilton and myself were being transferred.

"I started the season at Forest in great form. The first game of the season was against Southampton and I scored two goals in front of the television cameras. I had no idea then that it was going to be my last game.

"When I look back I would like to have stayed. Definitely. The only reason I can think of is finance. While I was injured the club brought in Ian Wallace and then Justin Fashanu arrived. They both cost £1m-plus, and they had built the Executive Stand so I wonder whether Forest had actually overspent. What other reason could there be even to consider allowing the likes of Shilton and myself to leave? I'd have liked to have stayed because I wanted to help Forest win more trophies and be considered as a bargain at £1m."

He need not worry too much. The next time Francis goes to that bank, opens the vault and dusts off the gold medal with 'Coupe Des Clubs Champions Europeens' written across the middle, he will know that he justified every last penny of that historic transfer fee. And much more besides.

# FOUR

# Garry Birtles

*He could do everything - hold the ball up, turn and run at defenders, score goals. Birtles was the best centre-forward I have ever seen. A fabulous, fabulous footballer.*

**Viv Anderson**

FORTY-TWO LEAGUE games unbeaten. Brian Clough cherished that record almost as much as the two European Cups. It was the ultimate sign of consistency in the English game - and beating Forest had become a national obsession.

When Liverpool finally managed it on December 9th, 1978, Clough marched on to the Anfield pitch at the final whistle to applaud his players off.

And then Arsenal came along. On August 22nd, 2004, they came back from 3-1 down against Middlesbrough to win 5-3 and extend their own unbeaten run to 42 games. Three days later they beat Blackburn 3-0 to wipe Forest from the record books. And the following morning Garry Birtles is sat in his front lounge making a remarkably bad job of being a good sport. "I should have made a voodoo doll of Thierry Henry," he muses. "Stuck some pins in." Not that he has anything against Arsene Wenger or Arsenal. "No, no, they're a fantastic team," he says. "But maybe they can start talking about being on our level when they have won the European Cup a couple of times."

Birtles speaks with a devotion to Forest that befits a man who was born and bred in Chilwell, educated at Alderman White School and, at home in Long Eaton, has black-and-white pictures of 1930s Wheeler Gate and Goose Fair hanging in his entrance hall.

If he sounds biased, it is because he probably is. Birtles is the type of guy who would have 'You've Lost That Loving Feeling' as his ringtone, a man who grew up with posters of Ian Storey-Moore and Joe Baker on his bedroom walls, dreaming that one day he could pull on that Garibaldi-red jersey.

He can still remember watching from the Trent End as Chris Crowe scored a hat-trick and George Best, Bobby Charlton and the rest of Manchester United's players were thrashed 4-1. And at the age of 18 he signed a petition at the Palais nightclub on Lower Parliament Street calling for Clough to be installed as Forest's manager. Ignoring, for one moment, the European Cups and Wembley triumphs, his dream came true the moment he signed from Long Eaton United in December 1976, for the princely sum of £2,000.

True to form, Clough never missed an opportunity to tell him he was over-priced. Yet Birtles developed into the quintessential Clough forward - strong in the air (despite being rake-thin), blessed with an exquisite first touch and famed for his indefatigable work rate. "I likened his contribution to our success with that of a dying man crawling through the desert then finding a spring of water," Clough said in *Forest - The 1979 Season*. "We were that desperate for goals when he came along."

A common misconception, however, is that Birtles had an immediate impact at the City Ground. The reality could hardly be more the opposite. True, Birtles had forced himself into the first team within three months, playing in midfield in a 2-0 win over Hull City, but it was to be his one and only league appearance in his first two seasons at the club. "If I ever play you in midfield again, tell the chairman to give me the sack," the silver-tongued Clough told him.

There was certainly no hint of what was to come when Birtles was relegated to the reserves, quickly becoming disheartened. He was ineligible for a championship winner's medal in 1978, and there were times when he wondered how he would ever get in the team ahead of Peter Withe and Tony Woodcock.

"In the first two years a summons from Clough usually meant one thing - and it wasn't a place in the first-team," he says. "I'd be on the training ground caked in mud when somebody would come down and haul me off early: 'Gaz, the Gaffer wants you over at

Trent Bridge for a game of squash.' I was his squash partner but there was no way he was going to select me ahead of Withe or Woodcock."

It was only when Withe fell out with Clough and left for Newcastle in August 1978 that Birtles finally seized his chance. Steve Elliott, who had been an apprentice at the club, initially assumed the number-nine jersey but Peter Taylor went into bat on Birtles's behalf and persuaded Clough to change his mind.

"Peter had been to watch me in a reserve game at Coventry. It was lashing down with rain and he didn't want anybody to know he was there so he paid to get in and sat in the corner of the stand with the collar of his jacket turned up.

"Until then Clough had always preferred Elliott but I used to do this little trick where I would drag the ball back. Pete saw me do it and that convinced him I had a future. So he persuaded the Gaffer it was time to give me a chance. Otherwise I'd probably never have got into the first team."

His First Division debut came at home to Arsenal - a match that also saw Gary Mills become the youngest Forest player ever to appear in the league, aged 16 years and 203 days. "I was terrified so God knows how he felt," says Birtles. "But we came out 2-1 winners. It was our first win of the season and Clough told me afterwards that I would stay in the team for the European Cup tie against Liverpool the following Wednesday. In other words I'd gone from the Central League to the European Cup in the space of a week."

September 13th, 1978, will be remembered as one of the most glorious nights in Forest's history. It was also the defining moment for Birtles, a night when he came of age and confirmed once and for all that he belonged in such exalted company.

Throughout the 1970s Liverpool were as hard to shift as that other red menace of the time, the Soviet Union. They had just beaten Tottenham 7-0 at Anfield and were trying to "do an Ajax" by retaining the European Cup for a third successive year. The consensus was that they would dismiss their English rivals as easily as picking off flies. But Forest had already beaten Liverpool in the League Cup final and taken "their" league title.

# DEEP INTO THE FOREST

"Liverpool were really tense. They didn't like us and they didn't care if we knew," recalls Birtles. "So when I prodded in Woodcock's pass to give us a half-time lead there were a few insults being thrown around.

"I'll always remember Phil Thompson running past me with five minutes to go: 'Don't think one goal will be enough,' he called over. Actually, he almost spat out the words. The message was: 'We'll sort you out at Anfield.' And they sorted out most people in those days. He was being deadly serious.

"I picked up the ball on the halfway line, headed towards the box, whipped my left foot around it and Woodcock headed it down at the far post for Colin Barrett to volley it in. Two-nil. Brilliant. I couldn't resist it. 'Will two be enough then?' I shouted as I ran past Thompson. And, just for once, he was rendered speechless.

"I couldn't believe I'd done it afterwards. Here I was, a complete upstart, trying to get one over on an England international and Liverpool legend. I'd played about two serious games before then. I was a whippersnapper compared to him but I made sure he heard me."

Most observers still felt Liverpool were capable of making up the deficit. Before the second leg a poll of the First Division managers revealed that 17 out of 20 thought Liverpool would qualify. Only Alan Dicks (Bristol City), John Neal (Middlesbrough) and Ken Shellito (Chelsea) put their faith in Clough's European novices. Yet Liverpool's reputation, which had loomed large over most European sides, mattered not to Forest. "So what?" was the collective reply to the famous "This is Anfield" sign.

Birtles says: "Most of the country were backing Liverpool but no one here thought we would lose. No one. I was a bit nervous before the match but that soon went. I looked around at my teammates and saw no fear. We knew what we had to do. Before the game we were just milling about on the pitch and someone in the Kop threw a tennis ball at John Robertson. Robbo just flicked it up and volleyed it into the goal. Top corner, too."

Robertson's improvisation earned a spontaneous round of applause but the mood soon turned poisonous as Forest, inspired by

Peter Shilton, held out for a scoreless draw. "The fans hated us up there. The atmosphere was as nasty as I've ever experienced at a football ground. My dad was in the Forest end and the Liverpool supporters were throwing everything they could get their hands on: darts, ball bearings, coins. So much for the loveable Scousers and their famous sense of humour. They were watching their European Cup hat-trick disappear."

Graeme Souness, a losing member of that Liverpool side, still appears to be wallowing in a vat of sour grapes. In a newspaper interview a quarter of a century later he described Forest as dour and defence-minded, saying there can be no comparison with Wenger's Arsenal.

Birtles looks aghast. "So a dreary side won back-to-back European Cups? Christ, how could anyone describe us as dreary? We had John Robertson on one side, Martin O'Neill on the other, Tony Woodcock in attack, Trevor Francis, need I go on? We were a bloody good side, full stop.

"I used to room with Terry McDermott on England duty and I know how highly he regarded Forest. It was the same with Kenny Dalglish, Mark Lawrenson and Alan Kennedy.

"The fact is we never got the credit we deserved. We just weren't fashionable enough for some people, I suppose. Or maybe it was sour grapes - the fact we had the Indian sign over Liverpool, for instance.

"If Souness thinks we were dull I might send him my Glory Years DVD. My daughter watched it recently and rang me up: 'Hey, respect Dad, how good were you lot?' I put it on and she was right - I couldn't believe how good we actually were. Some of the stuff Robbo was doing was just unbelievable. A genius, that bloke - the best crosser of the ball I've ever seen."

Birtles got on the end of many of those sumptuous Robertson deliveries. Wiry and athletic, visibly growing with confidence and possessing a wonderfully subtle left foot, he not only scored against Liverpool but followed it up with goals in every round of the European Cup to the final. Just as crucially, it was his flick-on from a Robertson corner that led to Ian Bowyer's stooping header beating Harald Schumacher, Germany's legendary goalkeeper, for the semi-final winner in Cologne.

# DEEP INTO THE FOREST

The nerves were back for the final against Malmo. "We were sitting in the garden of the team hotel, waiting for the bus to take us to the stadium, and Clough could tell I was terrified. I never had a beard back then - he never let me have one - but I always grew a bit of a shadow before a match. He knew that and he had never minded before. But this time was different. "He turned to me: 'Get up to that room and get shaved' was the command. It was bizarre. He provided the razor and Chris Woods had the aftershave. Everyone was waiting around while I had to go upstairs. But, again, there was method to his madness. He wanted to take my mind off the match and that 20 minutes calmed me down.

"There were two crates of beer on the bus to the ground as well. He was brilliant at that sort of thing."

Like everyone who has worked with Clough for any length of time, there were occasions when it led to a testy relationship between tutor and pupil. Yet he grew remarkably fond of Clough and his eccentricities - whether it was ordering the players to run through a field of nettles at the end of training or plying them with booze on the eve of their most important matches.

"The night before the League Cup final against Southampton in 1979 we were absolutely blotto. We were in a hotel with absolutely everything we could possibly want to drink - bitter, mild, lager, champagne - and there were people who could hardly stand when we went to bed. But Clough insisted on it. Archie Gemmill got up to go at one point and the Gaffer wouldn't let him leave the room. But it didn't do us any harm. We were 1-0 down at half-time but once we sobered up we were okay."

Birtles scored twice as Forest eventually ran out 3-2 winners. "Garry Gives Reds the Cup," was the headline in the *Nottingham Evening Post*. "Not bad considering I was on all fours when I climbed the stairs to bed the previous night," he muses.

Clough used the same ploy before the European Cup tie against Arges Pitesti in Romania in 1979. "It was an arsehole of a place - an afternoon match because they didn't have floodlights," says Birtles. "The night before we must have shared 16 bottles of wine. It relaxed us and we won 2-1. The dieticians at clubs these days would probably be appalled but it worked for us."

# GARRY BIRTLES

He leans back in his chair and smiles. His thoughts have turned to his old match-day preparations. "I used to have a massive fry-up every Saturday morning. Or a fillet steak for dinner if it was a midweek match. Can you imagine them doing that now? Arsene Wenger would have a funny turn just thinking about it.

"Another time I had sunk ten pints the night before a home match and was playing cards at a mate's house until two in the morning. I wouldn't recommend it, but we were in the middle of a terrible winter, it was minus-ten outside and the City Ground was iced over. The truth is I never thought the game would get the go-ahead. I kept waiting for the phone call on the Saturday morning but it never came. So I went in with an almighty hangover. I got the man-of-the-match award that day."

A couple of times Birtles tried to take Clough on but he soon learned the manager was not just unpredictable but unputdownable. "One of his tricks was to drag us away on strange trips abroad. We'd normally get about 24 hours' notice, come back jet-lagged, fed up and wondering why on earth we had put ourselves through it. I remember one Sunday morning getting a phone call telling me to be at the ground for nine o'clock because we were going to Kuwait. 'You bloody what?' I thought.

"I was injured so there was no way I could play and I'd been looking forward to Sunday lunch and a few pints at my local. So I got on the coach, sat at the back and started moaning to all the other lads.

"We set off for the airport but eventually Clough got a whiff of it: 'What's wrong with you?' he asked.

"I took a deep breath. 'You're taking me halfway round the world for a match I can't even play in - I'd be better off staying here and getting fit.'

"I could see that look in his eye. 'Son, you're absolutely right - Albert, stop this fucking bus.'

"This was on Wilford Lane. He jumped off the coach, flagged down the first car and popped his head through the window: 'Excuse me sir, can you take this young man back to the City Ground?' Then he bundled my case into the car and jumped back on the bus. The poor guy didn't know what had hit him. He was probably on his way to church and then Cloughie came out of nowhere. He stood no chance."

Peter Taylor could be just as unorthodox. "The guy was hilarious. But he was paranoid too. He was convinced we were being bugged. Before our team meetings he'd check the cupboards, look out of the windows, behind the sliding doors - he was terrified people were listening in.

"Before we played Ajax [the 1980 European Cup semi-final] he wanted us to be relaxed, so he took us into Amsterdam's red-light district and started bartering with the manager of a live sex show to get 17 of us in half-price.

"We ended up in a seedy little bar across the road from all the women in the brothel windows. Can you imagine Alex Ferguson doing that with Manchester United before a European Cup semi-final? It was bizarre, but I've always said we were probably the only team in the country would who would be fined if we didn't go out for a drink on a Friday night."

Trevor Francis was missing for the final (Forest beat Ajax 2-1 on aggregate) and Birtles was deployed as a lone target man, running himself into a frazzle. "I've never seen a lad cover as much ground, willingly and unselfishly, as Birtles did that night," Clough said afterwards. "Honestly, I've never seen a more exhausted footballer in all my time in the game."

Birtles finished the game with his socks round his ankles, scarcely able to jog let alone run. But his tackling back and scrapping for possession seemed to lift the entire team, never more so than in the 21st minute when he prodded the ball back to John Robertson to score the only goal of the game.

"Gary Mills had started in attack with me but after ten minutes Clough and Taylor realised we were going to get battered unless we went to 4-5-1," says Birtles. "I had to run my heart out and I was absolutely knackered by the end. I had a great chance to run clear late on but my legs were like treacle. I thought I was going to die.

"But I can remember getting the ball in the last few minutes and taking it to the corner flag. Kevin Keegan came running over to get it off me but I did a couple of circles and he gave away a free-kick. Keegan was so frustrated he picked up the corner flag and threw it to the floor. I enjoyed that. Then the famous Clough line afterwards was that I had done more miles than Emil Zatopek."

Without the contribution of their spindly striker, Forest might well have buckled under the near-unremitting Hamburg pressure. "They were throwing everything at us and then the referee finally blew the whistle," says Birtles. "The officials were carrying a table and the trophy on to the pitch and I was punching the air: 'YES, THAT'S IT, WE'VE WON IT!'

"And then the bloody ref was shouting that it was an offside. The ball was back in play and the two blokes with the trophy were scurrying off the pitch. I couldn't believe it. But we came through."

It feels like a trick of the imagination sometimes that four years earlier the teenage Birtles was working as an apprentice carpet-fitter in Chilwell with his father. Aston Villa had turned him down, despite persuading him to leave school at 15 for a month-long trial, and he had even considered abandoning football to try his luck as a professional squash player.

Then a friend of Peter Taylor's rang the City Ground to warn him he had heard a whisper that Manchester United might sign a young lad from Long Eaton. "I was thunderstruck - I expect that sort of information from my staff," Taylor wrote in *With Clough By Taylor*. "I phoned my scout for the area who said: 'Oh Birtles. Used to be at Clifton. Can't play.'

"I fumed: 'Whether he can play or not, if he goes to Old Trafford and signs, you'll get the sack'." Clough put Taylor in charge of a 1-0 defeat at Oldham while he went to see what all the fuss was about. "We were playing an FA Cup qualifying tie at Enderby Town," says Birtles. "It was my big chance but one of their guys split my shinpad with a shocking tackle and I was carried off.

"Clough said afterwards that the half-time Bovril was better than my performance but he came back to see me in a match at Burton Albion. We lost 4-0 but he gave me a month's trial and then signed me on.

"It was frightening sometimes. Roy of the Rovers stuff. I went from working on building sites, fitting carpets, smelling adhesive all day, to playing for my hometown club in European Cup finals.

# DEEP INTO THE FOREST

For a club of Forest's size, it was incredible - like Barnsley doing it these days. I was reading Phil Soar's history of Nottingham Forest and there was a quote from a German journalist, saying that of all the clubs to win the European Cup we were the greatest because of our background and how small we were. How true is that? And it all happened in the space of three years. Like I say, it was frightening at times."

Birtles scored 42 goals in his first two seasons as a first-team player. He won the club's player-of-the-year award in 1978/79 and was nominated for the Professional Footballers' Association young-player-of-the-year title won by Cyrille Regis of West Bromwich Albion.

"I would never have imagined getting so many goals," he admits. "There were times when I was pinching myself. It had taken so long to get in the team I was getting a bit disillusioned with things and I didn't really know which direction I was going.

"I started as an outside-left and I don't mind admitting I was lazy at times. I just used to stand on the wing and wait for the ball to come to me. I didn't really appreciate what was expected of me until Clough played me in midfield in the reserves. I had a lot more work to do there."

Unofficially, he was also the worst-dressed Forest player. "He appeared in all sorts of things," says Tony Woodcock. "At Forest he was into the baggy look, woolly trousers and jackets. I used to call him Charlie Chaplin." When England were knocked out of the European Championship in 1980 the team drowned their sorrows in an Italian nightclub. "Most of us were still in our England suits," recalls Woodcock. "Garry went up to get changed and came down in a yellow and black striped shirt, which he was wearing with a tie. When he walked in everyone just fell about.

"We thought that was bad enough but the next morning when we went to leave he capped it. It was fairly hot and we were all in casual shirts. Then Garry appeared in a heavy tweed and wool suit with a shirt and dicky bow. He must been sweating buckets. The more comments he got, the more outrageous he became."

Manchester United eventually prised the sartorially challenged Birtles away from his beloved Nottingham in October 1980, but only after their manager Dave Sexton had tabled a £1.25m bid, then a British record. Birtles had scored 66 goals in 162 appearances. "I didn't want to leave but I knew Manchester United were interested and then a magazine article appeared with Clough saying: 'I got Birtles this, I made his career, I bought his house, I paid for his car. . .'

"That really got me down. The fact was I must have been the lowest-paid player in the league at the time.

"My parents were upset too. It hurt all of us and there was no need for it, especially when I had done a good job for him. Manchester United were always my second team but I would have stayed if things had been right. Unfortunately they weren't, so I went to Old Trafford and had an absolute nightmare."

His loss of form in Manchester was shocking and mysterious. It took him almost a year to break his duck in the league and, football being an unforgiving workplace, he became the butt of jokes for music-hall comedians everywhere. One match report described his performance as "bordering on the statuesque" and in 2001 he merited a place in an *Observer* feature entitled: "The Top Ten Biggest Wastes of Money in Football."

"He was the 'great hope' when he came and most of us hung in with him as he tried to make his mark," recalls Tony Smith of Manchester United's *Red News* fanzine. "We longed for him to score a league goal because we shared his embarrassment."

The agony was not to end until September 1981. "He scored the winner against Swansea," says Smith. "Then he appeared on television the following day, humble enough to repeat some of the tiresome jokes. If anything showed Garry was probably too nice, that was it."

Eventually Ron Atkinson replaced Sexton and put Birtles out of his misery, selling him back to Forest for £300,000. "I'd say he left with no hard feelings," concludes Smith, remembering a pre-season open day at Old Trafford in 1981. "It featured a mock training session during which the first-team practised one-on-one situations against the goalkeeper. Poor Garry was even under pressure here and several thousand hearts were in mouths fearing he would still be unable to hit the net. Whether Gary Bailey was feeling generous, I don't know, but Birtles scored his meaningless shot and we all felt pleased for him. That's how bad it had become.

"I'd seen the writing on the wall at a training session at the Cliff. I was surprised to see Birtles playing in defence and it was awful. Maybe he didn't have the confidence to play as a striker, even in training, but he seemed really depressed and generally out on a limb. He wasn't playing well and after one misplaced pass I was shocked by the reaction of the United coach. The guy needed a lift but was simply told he was useless."

Birtles can laugh about it now, but he was so desperately depressed at one stage that there were nearly disastrous consequences.

"We had played against Everton away and once again I hadn't done too well. I was travelling back to Nottingham and all I could think about were all the things that were going wrong in my career.

"I'm not sure exactly where I was, somewhere between Macclesfield and Leek. All I know is that I wasn't concentrating properly, the rain was pouring down and suddenly I had veered across my lane, over another carriageway and off the road. I headed straight for a farmer's gate and by pure chance it was open. I ended up parked in the farmyard. But if something had been coming the other way I dread to think what would have happened. That really made me think. Things are never as bad as you think. There are more important things in life than football.

"It was a horrible time for me but there were two jokes going around that made me laugh. The first was that John Lennon would have survived if I had been the man who shot at him. The other was that the hostages in the American Embassy in Iran were set free and the first thing they wanted to know was whether I had scored yet.

"Even I could see the funny side. But when I heard Cloughie wanted me back I would have walked to Nottingham. I took a fifty per cent pay cut, from £800 to £400 a week, scored in my first match (a 2-0 defeat of Watford) and it felt as though I had never been away."

Birtles had another five seasons at Forest, during which he formed a potent partnership with Nigel Clough and, before that,

# GARRY BIRTLES

Peter Davenport, another striker who would have a torrid time after a big-money move to Manchester United.

He also showed an unexpected talent for playing in the centre of defence and Brian Clough, of course, had his squash partner back. "It was a bit difficult at times," says Birtles. "I didn't know whether to try to beat him, or even to dare to take a game off him. If he obstructed you, your first instinct would be to ask for a 'let' but then he would turn round: 'Do you want that again, son?'

"He was a good player but he cheated a bit. You'd weigh it all up. 'Nah, it's all right, Gaffer - you carry on.' I always had to lose and maybe that's why he liked playing with me so much."

Birtles was just four short of his century of Forest goals when he severed his ties with the club for a second time. Or to put it more accurately, they severed their ties with him.

"They simply told me in a letter that they weren't going to retain me. Thanks a bloody lot. It pissed me right off, to be honest. It was FA Cup final day in 1987, Coventry City against Tottenham Hotspur. I used to watch that match religiously but that year I felt too sick even to turn it on. I just took myself off and played golf.

"After everything I had done for the club I thought I deserved better than that. Much better. In fairness to Clough, he did admit once he'd got rid of me a season too early. But it shows what a cut-throat business football is."

Not that he harboured any bad feelings. When journalists phoned Birtles after Clough's death they found him "in bits" - almost unable to speak. "I thought he was indestructible," he said.

He has kept in touch with the Clough family and was paid the ultimate compliment when his old manager asked to be called 'Brian' rather than 'Gaffer'.

"The same honour was bestowed upon Robbo, too, but we both found it impossible. He was always 'Gaffer' to us," he says.

"He was a top man - I really mean that. He plucked me from obscurity and turned me into an England player with two European Cup medals. If he hadn't done that I'd probably still be a floor-layer.

"It used to baffle me when the likes of Kevin Keegan and Trevor Brooking would say they could never play for him. I'd think: 'Why on earth not?' He could give you things that no other manager would be capable of. How he never got the England job was an utter disgrace. The FA should be ashamed - they were scared stiff of him.

"And why was he never knighted? Brooking was. Alex Ferguson was. Bobby Robson was. It's the most pathetic decision I could ever think of. Is it because he threatened to take on the Establishment? If so, how come Mick Jagger was knighted? It's absurd - absolutely ridiculous."

These days Birtles is a regular fixture in the City Ground pressbox where he writes a column for the *Nottingham Evening Post* and, with his outspoken views, is a natural for Sky television and local radio.

It must be difficult at times. Football clubs can be sensitive creatures. When he predicted (correctly) that Forest would be embroiled in a relegation fight in 2003/2004 Paul Hart stuck the offending article on the dressing-room wall as a motivational tool for his players. And when Birtles pointed out that some supporters would question Joe Kinnear's appointment the new manager angrily rounded on "ex-players poncing a living off this club."

The toughest part must be faking impartiality. So Birtles does not even go through the pretence. "It's hypothetical, of course, but imagine Forest at their peak playing against Arsenal." He considers it for a second. "It would be close. But we would come out on top. The Gaffer would have made sure of it."

# FIVE

# John McGovern

*He was still playing at 35 and looked only 21. Whatever he did, even if he was having a bad time, he would still want to do the right thing: train hard and work hard, and never have a bad word to say about anyone.*

**Tony Woodcock**

JOHN MCGOVERN'S CRITICS would have you believe he played midfield like Les Dawson played the piano. Which is strange considering he is one of the most decorated footballers in the business. McGovern has enough medals to fill a removal van but there were times when Narked of Nottingham would complain he was in the team only because he was Brian Clough's 'blue-eyed boy'. The scepticism used to mystify Clough and, for that matter, Peter Taylor, the man who first spotted a 15-year-old McGovern running round a muddy field in Hartlepool "with a funny waddle".

True, McGovern never had the star qualities of Trevor Francis or Peter Shilton. He might not have been blessed with the skill of John Robertson or Tony Woodcock, and his love of fine food and T. S. Lowry paintings might not have fitted in with the laddish, Bovril-and-chips culture of 1970s football. Yet Clough and Taylor knew every detail about McGovern apart from his fingerprints. To them, he was a natural leader, a man of courage who led by example and whose attributes outweighed any perceived shortcomings.

He was an ideal, reliable man to have in midfield, winning possession, playing the simple pass and laying the foundations for the more eye-catching players to strut their stuff.

Were he blessed with Clough-like bullishness McGovern could embarrass any of his detractors by reeling off his list of honours:

two European Cups, two league titles, one Super Cup, one League Cup (he was injured for the 1978 final against Liverpool) and the Charity Shield. It is not his style, of course. But lest it be forgotten, Franz Beckenbauer is the only footballer in the world who has been a European Cup-winning captain more times than the man who now features on a website celebrating the life and times of "Montrose's local heroes." Just beneath the writer Hugh McDermaid and "one of the guys from the Average White Band."

How appropriate, too, that it should be McGovern who delivered the lasting eulogy at Clough's memorial service in Nottingham, and how typical of the man that he chose his words so elegantly. Was that a tear in his eye? There was definitely a lump in his throat as he stood on the balcony of the Council House surveying the thousands of Forest supporters shoehorned into the Old Market Square. "As far as I could see," he says of that emotionally charged September morning in 2004, "for every man, woman or child wearing red, there were at least two in green sweatshirts. Cloughie's green."

To analyse the Clough-McGovern relationship it is necessary first of all to identify the tragic backdrop to McGovern's upbringing. In 1960 his ex-paratrooper father was killed in a road accident while in Ghana to work on the Volta Dam. "I was 11 at the time but he had been working abroad for two years so I was nine the last time I saw him," he says. "I hero-worshipped my father. Whenever we won something I'd think to myself: 'Why can't he be here to see it?'"

McGovern was not looking for a substitute father but Clough had paternal instincts that thrust him into the role regardless. "As a young lad growing up without a father I was glad of someone like him to impose rules and look up to," says McGovern. "People say he was a father figure for me. I think 'mentor' is a better word. But whichever description you use, the fact is that I grew to worship him as well. I would have done anything for Brian and I owe him everything. I just feel grateful to have worked and lived alongside a genius."

It is easy to see why Clough felt so much for McGovern. In many ways he was the prototypical Clough man - courteous, clean-shaven, hardworking and conscientious. Clough did not like heroics. He wanted industrious players who would follow his instructions. Above all, he wanted his men to perform to the limits of their ability in every match. McGovern did just that and was rewarded with a career of near-unbroken success.

Sometimes Clough would ring him at home late on a Friday night, to check he was indoors and that his clean-cut image was not just a charade. Deep down, he knew that McGovern would answer every time. Apart from the occasional pint of Guinness, the midfielder was free of any vices. Indeed, it is difficult to imagine there could have been a more dedicated professional. Nobody lingered longer on the training ground, habitually staying on after the rest had gone, honing his skills and fuelling reserves of stamina second to none. Even when Clough plied his players with booze on mid-season breaks to Spain, McGovern was guaranteed to rise with the sun for a three-mile run every morning. "Habit," he said, whenever Clough quizzed him.

By his own admission, he was not far short of John Robertson as the slowest player at the club, but Clough knew he had pace in abundance elsewhere in the team. McGovern was a tenacious tackler and a capable passer who recognised his limitations while playing with utter self-belief. So why the resentment on the terraces?

"The fans thought I had an ugly style and they were right, although there was a good reason for it," explains McGovern. "When I was 28 I went for a medical examination and the doctor told me I had a muscle missing from my back. It meant I had an unusually rounded left shoulder and when I ran it held me back. I had no pace and an ugly running style. The fans wanted someone who was graceful whereas I always looked a bit awkward.

"It was a handicap, a quirk, call it what you like, and I found out about it too late to do anything about it. The medical people said they could break my shoulder and try to re-align everything but I was coming towards the later stages of my career by then.

"I can remember all the various descriptions, none of them too flattering. I was likened to a horse running through treacle - that was one of my favourites. Even my teammates got in on the act. Archie Gemmill once told me I looked as though I was running with a broken arm."

# DEEP INTO THE FOREST

Thankfully, McGovern was a sturdy enough character to cope when he heard the fans chanting the names of his teammates (serenading everyone, it seemed, but him) or noisily expressing their displeasure whenever he made a mistake.

Clough thought McGovern took to the holding midfield role like a fish to water. Others thought he looked more like a cat in water. "I'll never forget a director asking me why I had signed a 'sparrow-footed, innocuous, frail weakling'," Clough once said.

Lesser men may have crumbled but McGovern could always console himself that he had Clough's unreserved backing. "The fans never really took to me, wherever I played," he says matter-of-factly. "I got used to it in the end and it never bothered me because Brian saw things that others didn't and that was all that really mattered." Note the 'Brian'.

"Even the local paper in Nottingham didn't seem to like me," McGovern continues. "I don't know how they managed it but they failed to mention me in 12 successive match reports - and that was when we were winning. But as long as I was in the first-team I was happy enough. And I generally was. I had masses of respect for Brian and because of my commitment I like to think he showed me that respect back by picking me week in week out."

At times it felt as though Clough was deliberately championing a muck-and-nettles player ahead of more skilful teammates. Martin O'Neill remembers replacing the injured McGovern for the first leg of the 1980 Super Cup final against Barcelona. "I always wanted to play central midfield and I came off the pitch thinking I had done really well," he says. "Then Clough turned to me: 'Don't worry, you'll be back on the right when McGovern's fit.'"

According to a letter - entitled 'In Praise of McGovern' - in a match-day programme from the 1978/79 season, many of the boo-boys "usually decide what sort of game John will have before he has even tossed up."

Yet the cynicism of some supporters astonished McGovern's admirers throughout the game. "I'll always remember when we beat Cologne 1-0 in the second leg of the 1979 European Cup semi-final. In the papers the following day Gunter Netzer, who had been at Borussia Moenchengladbach and Real Madrid and had been a magnificent midfielder for Germany for many years, gave me one of the greatest compliments I have ever had.

"To quote him accurately, he said: 'Who is this McGovern? I had never heard of him - yet he was running the midfield.'

"I didn't keep that newspaper cutting but maybe I should have done. To have someone like him being so fulsome in his praise actually shocked me. It's the sort of accolade that every player craves. After that, you don't worry about the supporters so much. I couldn't have wished for higher praise."

The compliments were not always so forthcoming from Clough, who never spared McGovern from his acerbic asides. "I came off the field one time, feeling pretty pleased with myself after a good display against Alan Ball of Everton, and Brian singled me out to say well done. The sting came a few seconds later: 'You did well, young man, because he's a good player - and you're not.'

"People say I was his blue-eyed boy and all that sort of stuff but the fact is I probably got as many rollickings as anyone. Even when I was in my mid-20s he would have me doing tasks that the groundstaff would usually be in charge of. People say he mellowed with age but he could still terrify me."

Despite the occasional verbal swipe, Clough's regard for McGovern can be measured simply by the fact he signed him four times in a decade. No other player worked for Clough for longer. "And I could have been with him at five clubs," points out McGovern. "I turned him down when he took over at Brighton after leaving Derby. When I told him I preferred to stay where I was, he slammed the phone down on me."

The one thing that Clough could not give McGovern was full international recognition and, though he won two Scottish under-23 caps, he was never promoted to the senior squad. Not even Clough could argue too vehemently against McGovern's exclusion in an era of Billy Bremner, Graeme Souness, Asa Hartford, Don Masson and, of course, Archie Gemmill but there was little doubt he felt his trusted lieutenant was the equal of his rivals.

"Having known me from when I was at school, he understood what kind of character I was," says McGovern. "Most of all, he knew the honesty and commitment I gave him was everything I'd got. There wasn't any 90 per cent about it. Whenever I went out it was 100 per cent commitment and nothing less - whether I was playing well or playing badly. And if things were going badly I would never hide. If my form dipped, Brian knew that with my commitment it would quickly be corrected."

Their long association began one Sunday morning in Hartlepool at a don't-call-us, we'll-call-you trial for the town's junior footballers. McGovern was 15 and had turned up on his bike. "I had only started playing football a year earlier. I was captain of the school's rugby and cricket teams but I was still new to football and my school didn't even like me playing it. But I must have done something to impress Brian and Peter Taylor because they locked the gates and told me they would not open them until I had agreed to sign."

One problem. McGovern attended the strict, rugby-only Henry Smith Grammar school where, to put it bluntly, the headmaster considered football to be to sport what athlete's foot is to injuries.

The school wanted McGovern to go to university and abhorred the idea that one of its boys would want to join a scruffy Fourth Division football club. "The headmaster despised football and he had me stood up in his office for an hour reeling off all the reasons why I shouldn't want to play it.

"To play a sport that wasn't associated with the school was something the headmaster was totally against and he told me that in no uncertain terms. What he didn't realise was that I had already made up my mind. But Brian had his work cut out to persuade the headmaster otherwise. He had to turn on his full charm because I wouldn't have been allowed if the school had not signed forms giving me permission."

Clough had compromised, allowing him to study two days a week at West Hartlepool Further Education College. McGovern became the first apprentice at Hartlepool - or Hartlepools, as it was known back then - and when he broke into the side at the end of the 1964/65 season he was the youngest player on their books, still five months short of his 17th birthday.

McGovern was immediately taken aback by Clough's imposing manner. "He was very strict and it didn't suit all the players. But it was fine as far as I was concerned because my mother had brought me up in a strict fashion. I was well-disciplined and well brought up, and I thrived on his style.

"Sometimes he would say something to you in the manner of a parent talking to a small child but there would always be an explanation and he was always right.

"His first instructions to me were: 'Stand up straight, put your shoulders back and get your hair cut - you look like a girl.' I was terrified - I never wanted to see him again as long as I lived.

"I was a Rolling Stones fan and, like many boys of that age, I wanted to be the next Mick Jagger so I'd grown my hair like him. I fancied myself as a singer and three of us from school would hang around together with a harmonica, a drum and a guitar. But Brian was having none of it.

"I plucked up the courage to say: 'George Best has it styled this way.'

"His answer was simple: 'When you can play like George Best I'll let you have it that way. Now get it cut.' I had it trimmed at first but I soon had it cut short. Like he liked it. There was no compromise."

Who would have thought then that the Rolling Stones wannabe would become one of the most decorated footballers in the game's history? In 13 years under Clough's tuition, McGovern went on to be photographed with every trophy available at club level apart from the FA Cup. As he said in that emotive eulogy from the balcony of the Council House: "If I ever need memories of Brian I just have to look at my medal cabinet - it's full of them."

At Derby, having signed from Hartlepool for £7,500, McGovern scored the goal in a 1-0 defeat of Liverpool that effectively won Clough's team of McFarland, Mackay and Hinton the 1972 league title.

Yet his allegiance to Clough was always going to work against him when they teamed up again at Leeds United, particularly when he was asked to operate in place of Billy Bremner, the local hero. The fans despised Clough and took it out on his favourite player. McGovern's every touch was booed and the criticism from the terraces was so vitriolic he eventually went into the match-day programme. "The more you jeer the harder I'll try," he wrote.

It never turned out that way. Once Clough had been sacked the 25-year-old McGovern became *persona non grata* at Elland Road, as did John O'Hare, who had signed with him in a £150,000 joint deal from the Baseball Ground. They were Clough's men and, as such, were never going to fit in.

"Brian was there for 44 days but I had to stick it out for seven months," says McGovern. "I was a square peg in a round hole. I tried to make the most of it but, having my links with Clough, I was never going to make any progress as far as the first-team was concerned."

He had to have selective hearing so strong were the anti-Clough sentiments in the dressing room. "They were so brazen about it, that's what got me. There were times when Brian was manager and the players would have meetings to talk about how to get rid of him. I would just sit there at the back not saying anything. But what did they think I'd be thinking? Honestly, by the time Brian contacted me to go back to Forest I'd have gladly walked down the motorway."

To Clough's eternal pleasure, he had to pay only £60,000 to re-sign McGovern and O'Hare who, between them, had managed no more than ten league appearances at Leeds. McGovern was quickly installed as captain and Clough wasted little time in telling the up-and-coming Viv Anderson, John Robertson and Tony Woodcock to take their example from the new signing.

"I've bought him to show the others how to play," said Clough. There then followed a five-year period that could have had Roy of the Rovers checking with his copyright lawyers. "People always ask about the European Cups and, don't get me wrong, that was a truly fabulous achievement but for me, as captain, winning the league in our first season in Division One meant more," says McGovern. "In the cups you can be lucky in certain rounds but if you are top of the league after 42 games there's no disputing that you are the best team.

"We were champions of England, and deservedly so. Then people were looking at us thinking, yes, they've won their

# JOHN McGOVERN

domestic league but can they prove they're the best team in Europe as well? And we proved for two years that we were better than anyone else. We went out and won the lot."

Even for someone with his serene nature it is a source of constant irritation that, outside the East Midlands, so many people have selective memories when it comes to categorising the great sides from the different eras.

McGovern, it might not surprise you, has done his mathematics. He has worked out that Forest won 78 per cent of their European Cup matches from 1978 to 1980, whereas Manchester United won only 68 per cent of theirs in the two-year period that culminated in Sir Alex Ferguson's team returning the trophy to Old Trafford in 1999. And it still rankles that Forest did not even make the top 20 of a poll to find the best teams of all time, especially as the Liverpool side of 1979 made it to number 12. The same Liverpool team, of course, that Forest knocked out of the European Cup in the first round without conceding a goal over two legs.

"Brian Clough's great trick was making the game simple for players, and supplying them with the confidence and the self-belief that he possessed to the same levels as Muhammad Ali. But he needed players with the talent to carry out his instructions. Sometimes it gets forgotten just how good the players at Forest were.

"We were presented as a ragtag and bobtail bunch, but that was nonsense. John Robertson was a genius, the best player in Europe without a doubt, Peter Shilton was the best goalkeeper in the business and Kenny Burns was voted England's player-of-the-year.

"Unfortunately we still never get the credit we deserved. We had an inspirational manager but the so-called experts describe us as a team of odds and sods, and even worse sometimes. What on earth are they talking about? Are they seriously trying to say John Robertson, Peter Shilton, Kenny Burns, Archie Gemmill, Garry Birtles, Tony Woodcock and Viv Anderson were odds and sods? They were all internationals, for starters.

"We weren't a massive club - but that very fact is what made our achievements even more remarkable. If anything, we should have been given more recognition because of where we had come from."

One game in particular stands out. "We went to Old Trafford and won 4-0 in December 1977. That didn't happen then and it doesn't happen now, but we pulled it off. It should have been ten as well. Seriously. We were going on a mid-season break to Benidorm the following week and Brian had warned us beforehand that we'd get no spending money if we didn't win. Well, we absolutely annihilated them."

And the European Cup finals? McGovern twice had his hands on that 17lb hunk of silverware, but on both occasions there was only a flicker of a smile. Why had he looked so serious? "I was thinking of my dad. My mother was there to enjoy it all but when I stood there and lifted the trophy I was just wishing my dad could have been there to share the moment. Whenever I lifted any trophy the sense of jubilation was always delayed because my thoughts would turn to him. But I can assure you I felt the proudest man in the world. When you've won a trophy like that you feel like you could lift it with one hand and take on Mike Tyson with the other. Honestly, you could put an elephant in the trophy and you'd still be able to lift it."

His abiding memory is the reception at East Midlands airport after the defeat of Malmo in 1979. "It was just a sea of red. Being the captain, I had the responsibility of looking after the trophy as we carried it through the crowds and I'll never forget the joy on everyone's faces."

And Clough's reaction? "He always kept his emotions in check and never let us see what he was thinking. His first words to us in the dressing room were typical of Brian. He simply told us we were entitled to go out for the night to celebrate but he still wanted us to look like a proper team when we arrived back in England next day. In other words he didn't want us turning up at the airport looking like a bunch of tramps.

"Believe it or not, though, because of the high standards we had set ourselves we were actually disappointed that we had not put on a better show and scored a few more goals. Malmo set out their stall to defend doggedly, with nine or ten players behind the ball, and they made it impossible for us to open up the game."

# JOHN McGOVERN

There is a certain irony (or maybe it was just logic?) that McGovern, having devoted his career to the Clough-Taylor alliance, should be forced out of Forest as a victim of their managerial split.

It was the 1981/82 season and Forest's declining fortunes could be encapsulated by a 3-1 home defeat to Third Division Wrexham in the FA Cup. Clough and Taylor were beginning to feel the pressures of two disappointing seasons and the wind of change was blowing through the City Ground. Taylor, a man devoid of sentimentalism, fixed his sights on McGovern and put him on the transfer list. Clough was appalled and promptly took him off it the following day. Eventually, McGovern was forced to realise his seven years at the City Ground were coming to a thoroughly unsatisfactory climax and left on a free transfer for Bolton Wanderers, whom he subsequently went on to manage.

To most observers, McGovern would have fitted the identikit as having all the attributes to become a successful manager in his own right, but it was to be a chastening experience.

At Bolton there is a story that, Clough-like, he ordered a young Peter Reid to shave. Unfortunately he did not have his old manager's messianic authority - or anything close. He had a spell as Peter Shilton's assistant at Plymouth Argyle, but walked out after falling out with him over money.

Then he teamed up with Archie Gemmill at Rotherham, but they lost more than they won. Eventually he became disillusioned with the way footballers no longer seemed to take their profession as seriously as they once did. "When I went into management I tried to sign players like myself," he explains. "I wanted people who were honest, dedicated and willing to give 100 per cent commitment. And it wasn't easy finding them, I can tell you. I'll always remember talking to Graeme Souness about the commitment of players when he was manager of Glasgow Rangers. He said some of his players wouldn't have got into the reserves at Liverpool or Forest when we were in our heyday. That was the problem I faced."

It feels cruel to point out that some Forest fans did not believe he was worthy of a place in the reserves either. He probably knows that, anyway. Certainly it is not lost on him when, working for BBC Radio Nottingham or on the after-dinner circuit, he hears fans describing him as a 'legend'.

"Twenty-five years on, you never have a bad game, do you?" he says, deep with irony.

His legacy is the pictures of him lifting the European Cup in the direction of Forest's euphoric travelling supporters, in Munich and Madrid. Equally, a younger generation of supporters will remember him as the man who paid such a moving tribute to Clough in the Old Market Square.

Clough had liked him as a footballer and a person and McGovern's speech was simple and effective. "The last time I stood on this balcony," he began, "we had brought back a very large gold cup from Europe [applause]. Brian was a teacher. He taught players how to pass the ball and told them to keep the ball on the floor and to respect authority. He was one of the greatest teachers the game has ever seen."

He finished with that famous Clough-ism, "be good", and then he was off to the City Ground for the match against West Ham and a parade of ex-Forest stars with their trophies. McGovern, typically, had been instrumental in arranging it. Just as he is every time there is an old-boys' get-together.

That day, watching him lead everyone out of the tunnel, raising both arms to salute the fans as he strode towards the centre circle, it was difficult to imagine how anyone could ever have disliked John McGovern.

# SIX

# Viv Anderson

*Normally when you call someone a model professional
it's a load of rubbish. In Viv's case it was absolutely true.*

**Martin O'Neill**

VIV ANDERSON IS ONE of those guys you hear before you see.
Remember Dom Joly's character in *Trigger Happy*? The bloke
with the mobile phone the size of a coffin. Anderson is not quite
that noisy but, even in the most secluded corner of the Griffin pub
in Bowdon, just south of Manchester, it is fair to say everyone
knows he is around. "I was a bit quieter in the old days, I must
admit," he says. And then he laughs that booming, infectious
laugh, and the glasses at the bar shake again.

The original plan had been to invite Anderson back to the estate
in Clifton where he grew up, to see the streets where he first played
jumpers-for-goalposts football and the playing fields where one of
Matt Gillies' scouts, Ernie Roberts, told him he could have a career
at his local club.

Yet Anderson lives in Cheshire now and as a former Manchester
United player the Griffin, he explains, is his favourite haunt. I am not
surprised. It was here that the likes of Bryan Robson, Paul McGrath
and Roy Keane used to embark on some of the epic benders for which
United's 'drinking school' were once infamous. Keane tells a story
about being in here on crutches, with his bad leg propped up on a bar
stool, when a *Manchester Evening News* reporter rang to ask how his
rehabilitation was going. "Fine, thanks - putting some hard work in,"
he replied, silently gesturing to the barmaid to set up another round.

True to form, the first person I see, among the 'Cheshire set'
blondes and rich college girls with their Louis Vuitton handbags, is
Norman Whiteside. Which is funny because he was in exactly the

same place the only other time I have been here. In fact, I later find out he is as much a part of the Griffin's furniture as the jukebox.

It is only when I am at the bar that a hearty guffaw over my right shoulder and that familiar Nottingham lilt informs me that Vivian Alexander Anderson, in his late-40s but looking considerably younger, is already here, too. Not that he is a loudmouth, or anything like one. It's just that he has one of those gregarious personalities that fill the room.

As Sir Alex Ferguson said once: "Everyone in football knows Viv."

All of which is a far cry from the shy, gawky teenager whom Brian Clough dropped within four days of taking charge at Forest, complaining that he was "too quiet for his own good."

Clough's first impression was of a raw novice with plenty of talent but precious little confidence in it. Martin O'Neill remembers Anderson being painfully self-conscious because of his skin colour. Others simply put it down to adolescent shyness. Whatever the truth, in Clough's twisted yet brilliant logic axing Anderson was the best way to toughen him up. "Walk tall or walk out," he told the young defender.

"He hadn't even been there a week and he left me at home," recalls Anderson, once he has made his excuses to Whiteside. "It was an FA Cup replay at Tottenham and I'd come off with cramp in the first match. That was his first day at the club and I don't think it went down well because he took Tony Woodcock to the replay instead of me. I can remember thinking to myself that the writing might be on the wall and that I wasn't going to be around long while he was in charge."

Perhaps the young Anderson would have been filled with more confidence had he known that, during his infamous 44-day spell as Leeds United's manager, Clough had actually tried to sign him in a cash-plus-player exchange for Terry Cooper.

As it was, he need not have fretted too much. Not only did he swiftly convince Clough he was a sturdy enough character to be an automatic first-team choice at the age of 20, becoming an integral part of the European Cup-winning teams and the first black footballer to play for England, he survived some bewilderingly rapid changes in personnel to remain under Clough for another nine years.

# VIV ANDERSON

In the early days Anderson could be crushed by one of Clough's put-downs. It is also sad to report their relationship had suffered significant damage before he left Forest to replace Pat Rice at Arsenal in 1984. But he is indebted too to the way Clough turned him from a reserve player in the old Second Division into a history-maker, winning enough medals in the process to fill an aircraft hangar.

"To play for your hometown club, win the league and then two European Cups, how do you get better than that?" he asks, leaning back in his chair.

"Clough helped us to achieve what we would have thought was unachievable. And it'll never be done again. It was a period of time that was unique."

His memories are mostly parochial but when he looks back at his 12 years with the club he is acutely aware that coming from an era of Alf Garnett 'comedy', when there was no 'Kick Racism out of Football' campaign and the National Front used to regard football matches as being ripe for recruitment, his impact on the game stretched far beyond the City Ground.

Given Clough often loved to play the role of the Englishman Abroad it is fair to assume Anderson might have had to opt for selective hearing amid the industrial language and speak-first-think-later taunts that are prevalent in any dressing room, particularly in those days when the sight of a black man playing football was considered a break from the norm.

But there were many times, as well, when Clough was demonstrably supportive of his player. If he suspected a rival had whispered a racist insult in Anderson's ear he would be out of his dugout, telling him to kick his opponent and "call him a white bastard" - hardly a hands-across-the-nations gesture, but meant well all the same.

One time when Anderson was a substitute at Carlisle his touchline warm-up was conducted to a backdrop of unremitting abuse. When a shaken Anderson got back to the dugout Clough demanded to know why he had done his exercises with his back to the crowd. "Get back out there and face them," Clough told him, wagging a finger.

# DEEP INTO THE FOREST

It would be an exaggeration to say Anderson grew immune to the taunts but it reached the stage where he could handle it, like the occasion when Celtic's notorious 'Jungle' started barracking him during the Uefa Cup tie at Parkhead in 1984. Not only did Anderson pointedly look straight at his tormentors, as if to demonstrate they could not faze him, he even had the temerity to take a bow.

"I remember that Carlisle game, in particular, because they were throwing bananas at me," he says. "I tried to ignore it and sat back down beside Clough in the dug-out as quickly as I could. He said: 'I thought I told you to warm up.' So I told him what was happening and he told me: 'You get back out there and warm up again.' In that respect he was very, very good.

"There were a few other things and the culture was very different then. But over a period of 20-odd years I can remember only three incidents, and they were all dismissed very quickly.

"I never had it that bad. It was a lot easier for me than, say, Laurie Cunningham or Cyrille Regis. Because they were forwards and flamboyant they were identified much more than me.

"I think Cyrille got a bullet through the post with a message: 'This one's for you if you play for England.' I never got anything like that because rather than scoring goals and getting all the headlines I just used to boot people. My job was just to kick the winger and try to run forward."

Booting people? Anderson does himself a disservice. If anything, he was a footballer ahead of his time - a cultured, overlapping wingback with an assured touch not usually associated with English defenders. There were few right-wingers, let alone full-backs, capable of making the penetrative bursts along the touchline for which Anderson became renowned, evading his opponents with those marvellously leggy surges and the characteristic knees-up style that was once likened to a man hurdling invisible trip wires.

Defensively, too, not many left-wingers relished coming up against a man whose telescopic legs and loping style earned him the nickname 'Spider' and made him such a formidable opponent.

# VIV ANDERSON

An England call-up was just a natural progression. "Yellow, purple or black - if they're good enough I'll pick them," Ron Greenwood, the England manager, had said as he announced Anderson's inclusion in the squad to face Czechoslovakia at Wembley in November 1978.

Anderson remembers this as the beginning of a ten-day period when television cameras from all over the world converged on 121 Rivergreen, the modest semi-detached house in Clifton where he had grown up. The press had been speculating for weeks that it could happen and it had even been billed as a three-way race between Anderson, Cunningham or Regis.

In the media frenzy that followed it was here that Forest's fans learned (doubtless to their disappointment) there were none of the stories that accompanied the meteoric rise of another local boy, Garry Birtles. Whereas Birtles had watched Forest from the children's enclosure of the Trent End, and once signed a petition calling for Clough to be appointed as manager, Anderson was revealed as a Manchester United fan who had been reduced to tears when, at the age of 16, they sent him a letter of rejection. Perhaps the men in power at Old Trafford also considered him too bashful. Whatever the reason, they could have saved themselves the £250,000 they paid Arsenal to sign him some 14 years later.

To the media, no detail was considered insignificant. Newspapers and magazines devoted page after page to the black boy from the predominantly white neighbourhood, how he had worked briefly as a printer and how Sheffield United had also rejected him before the keen-eyed Roberts asked him if he wanted a trial a little closer to home.

Great swathes of print examined the social make-up of Clifton, Anderson's integration into school life, from Bluebell Infants to Greencroft Middle and Fairham Comprehensive, and the differing reactions he had encountered in football, from his Forest debut in a 3-2 defeat of Sheffield Wednesday in 1974 to his teenage days with Clifton Athletic, Mallorca FC and Attenborough Colts.

Suddenly everyone wanted to know how, 24 years earlier, his father Audley had arrived in Plymouth on a boat from Jamaica, bringing with him nothing more than a couple of addresses in his top pocket, how the proud West Indian had got work as a porter at Nottingham's general hospital and how his wife Myrtle had followed him five months later, getting a job at the city's Highbury Hospital.

The television cameras even filmed Audley clambering into his Caravette to start the journey to Wembley (Myrtle could not get off the night-rota), but the truth is that their eldest son was never truly at ease with all the fuss.

To put it simply, Anderson's thoughts were not about inspiring millions of black kids across the world but about more basic matters, not least preventing the Czech left-winger getting over any crosses. And, as if faintly embarrassed by all the exposure, he has spent the last quarter of a century trying to play down the significance of the occasion.

"If you're a black civil rights leader in Brixton don't come to me," he once said. "If I became involved in that it would be a false image of me. In Toxteth, Brixton or Tottenham they probably have grievances, but I've been lucky. My parents have always looked after me. There is nothing false about me and it would be wrong for me to preach about this, that and the other when I've had no experience of it. Garth Crooks might be into that but I'm not and I don't feel guilty about it. I know my limitations.

"Peter Taylor said I was the ideal leader of a black revolution in football when I made my debut for England. I never understood that. What am I an example of exactly? Being able to kick a ball better than a lot of other people for ninety minutes on a Saturday afternoon, that's the limit of my example to people.

"The only reason I want to do better is for myself, not because I'm black or because people on the terraces are giving me stick. I want to become a better player and I don't consider that attitude a sell-out to my race. I'm a footballer doing a job so I want to do well for myself, my family, my manager and my team. That's all."

In the harsh environment of working-class football Anderson had made the decision early in his life that if he worried about every insult or funny look he would not have a long career. And who can blame him?

# VIV ANDERSON

"Being the first black England international, people were always going to make big things of it," he says. "At the time I just wanted to play football and not have to worry about the rest of it. I wanted to be in the next squad and the squad after that, and that was all I really cared about.

"I was a footballer not a politician. It's only now, more than 25 years on, that I realise what a big thing it was. My parents were on every television channel and I was getting telegrams from everyone from Laurie Cunningham's mum to Elton John and the Queen. I mean, that doesn't happen every other day.

"Even now, whenever any sort of race issue comes up everybody in the media is on the phone to me. But back then my attitude was: I just want to play football. Others could make of it what they want but I was more interested in doing well for the team."

Anderson's attitude could be accurately gauged in a 1978 interview with the *Guardian*, which began: "His look of mild amusement says it all: 'Why is this reporter going on about Martin Luther King, Muhammed Ali, Pelé, ethnic groups and racial prejudice when I'd rather stick to talking about football?'"

As Andrew Longmore, author of Anderson's excellent biography, puts it: "The significance of the occasion for young Anderson was never that he was leading a black revolution against the palace of the Football Association at Lancaster Gate but that he was getting a chance to establish himself as a regular international.

"That he also happened to be the object of national attention was one of those accidents of history, a case of being in the right place at the right time. Or perhaps the wrong place at the right time, because it is arguably Anderson's misfortune that he will not be remembered for his ability as a footballer, not for his one League Championship, two European Cup and three League Cup medals, not for his 30 or so international caps, but for his colour.

"Like it or not, when he walked out of the Wembley tunnel to be greeted by a crowd of 92,000 the tall, slim figure was bearing the standard for black people in Britain. Recognition? Yes. A new generation? Yes. Acceptance? Well, it was a start."

# DEEP INTO THE FOREST

Modest and affable, Anderson now features on the 100 Great Black Britons website, was awarded the MBE in 2000 and was inducted into the National Football Museum's hall of fame in Preston in November 2004.

He has also taken part in football workshops in Soweto as a "goodwill ambassador" for the Football Association and modestly tells the story of walking through Nottingham city centre with Ian Bowyer, unaware they were being followed by two young black boys. "Don't you realise you are idolised by the whole coloured population of the city?" Bowyer asked him. "You represent something which gives pride to them all."

Yet Anderson remains conspicuously more at ease reminiscing about moments of collective triumph rather than his own groundbreaking status. "When I look back now they were the times of my life," he recalls of that period from 1977 to 1980 when Forest supplanted Liverpool as the country's premier team. "I'll always remember we were on the bus coming away from the stadium after the first European Cup final and Frank Clark, who was in his mid-30s, was telling us: 'It doesn't get any better than this - just remember that everyone.'

"We just thought: 'yeah, yeah, shut up you old bastard.' But he was right. You don't appreciate it at the time. You just think we'll go and win it next year and the next year after that. You don't properly realise that most players go through their careers without winning anything."

So what was the secret to success? "Everything just clicked. You couldn't say there was one thing that triggered it off because it was a combination of many things. Everyone knew their job and Clough instilled in everyone what he wanted them to do every Saturday afternoon. And don't forget he inherited the likes of me, Tony Woodcock, Martin O'Neill and John Robertson. Okay, we weren't household names, but we all went on to become internationals.

"So Clough was lucky in one respect because he was inheriting good players rather than also-rans. Add to that the discipline he brought with him and the players he signed such as Trevor Francis, Peter Shilton, Kenny Burns, Larry Lloyd and it just gelled.

# VIV ANDERSON

"But the funny thing was that, tactically, Clough was actually incredibly basic. Later on in my career at other clubs I was given huge folders about the opposition and dossiers about each player I would be facing.

"There were never any team-talks under Clough except: 'That's the football, you keep it more than they do and you'll win.' His philosophy was that it was a very simple game and there were too many people in football trying to confuse it.

"There was a great team spirit, too, and I think Cloughie encouraged that. When I was at Arsenal you would try to organise something but one player lived one side of London, maybe an hour and a half away, and the next player would live the opposite side, two hours away. At Forest we'd all go out en masse, with our girlfriends and wives. We were one big group. Always."

Anderson remembers Clough and Peter Taylor as the classic police-state interrogators - the 'Gaffer' who could be a merciless bully and did not mind who he upset and 'Pete,' the more sympathetic type who would share a joke and lighten the mood.

"When it came to personal matters I got on better with Pete. It was like good-cop bad-cop with them, and Pete was the good one. All the lads would probably say the same thing.

"Cloughie came in like a whirlwind. He was a fantastic manager and he really got the best out of you. He was good at cajoling people, building up players, bollocking them, whatever it took to get the best out of them. He was truly excellent at it. But he was not the person you'd ring if you were going out for a pint. He was the last person you'd ring, really. But he taught us how to conduct ourselves on and off the field and I will forever be indebted to him."

He recalls a typical Clough episode. "It was the middle of the afternoon and I got a phone call saying can you come to the office, the manager wants to see you. Mark Proctor was there, too - he'd had exactly the same call.

"So the manager sat us down and explained he wanted us to go on loan to Derby to help out Pete Taylor, who was manager there at the time. A Nottingham lad going to Derby? It was just a no-no. Mark's from the North-east but he was as against it as me. We got our heads together. 'Nah, don't think so,' we both said.

"But Clough insisted: 'Well, you're going to have to tell Pete to his face.' He practically kidnapped us, bundled us into his car and drove to Pete's house at Widmerpool. Pete then went through the spiel about how great it would be to have us but I wouldn't budge. I told him: 'Pete, I'd love to for you, but the answer's no'.

"Mark said exactly the same and Cloughie was furious. He stormed off shouting: 'That's it then - you can get yourself home.'

"So it's the middle of nowhere, in the middle of winter, and we're stranded. We asked Mrs Taylor to call us a cab but it never turned up. So we had no choice but to walk home, through the fields, up and down these country lanes, knocking on doors at coming up to midnight, trying to get someone to get us another taxi. Surprise, surprise, Clough had us in the A-team the next day.

"But that was how he was - a strange, strange man. Nobody could work him out. You didn't know from one minute to the next what was going to happen.

"The team-sheet went up one afternoon for an evening match and I was in the starting line-up, so I came back in as usual, got my kit on and he turned round to me: 'I've changed my mind.'

"He pointed at one of the subs: 'Give him your kit, he'll do a better job than you tonight.' I pointed out I was already kitted out and he replied: 'I'm not bothered. Get your kit off.' I wasn't even a sub that night."

I ask whether he ever answered back and immediately feel stupid as his eyes widen, half incredulous at the prospect and half sympathetic to the innocence of his interviewer.

"What? Absolutely no chance! Repeat: no chance! No, no, no, no, no. He ruled by fear, as far as I'm concerned, especially in the early days. When you get a bit older there would be an element of: 'yeah, whatever Gaffer!' but he always had respect from everyone, young and old.

"Very few people answered him back and even fewer got away with it. Larry Lloyd tried it and it cost him a lot of money. The manager would fine you two weeks' wages, as simple as that."

# VIV ANDERSON

He recalls a European excursion when he had persuaded Tony Woodcock, John Robertson and Garry Birtles to break a curfew and slip into town for a few crafty drinks. "Robbo got as far as the reception but he couldn't manage those last few steps. He just clung to the door saying: 'I daren't, I daren't.' We tried to talk him round but he wouldn't have any of it."

Anderson never confronted Clough's idiosyncrasies with the same righteousness as Lloyd because he was a far more laid-back character, but their relationship was tempestuous enough for the manager, in Taylor's words, to "have no time for Viv" and consider him a "problem player" towards the end of their working relationship.

That did not prevent Clough trying to persuade Anderson out of going through with his £220,000 move to Arsenal. Clough was widely said to have decided the defender had passed his best but that does not tally with the account of Anderson who recalls his manager lecturing him with the old line that "the grass is greener in Nottingham" and asking why he would ever want to move to London.

By that stage, however, Forest's right-back was no longer an easy touch who could be ordered around and bullied. At 28, Anderson could still be over-awed by Clough but it had reached the stage where he had heard all his one-liners before. There were signs, too, that Clough had lost his inspirational touch in the transfer market.

Added to that, he felt Clough had betrayed his players during their run to the Uefa Cup semi-finals. "We never got the bonuses that had been promised," he explains. "We'd trusted him all the way throughout. He'd told us: 'If we do well, I'll look after you, don't worry about that.' But we got through to the last four to play Anderlecht and didn't get a penny."

If only the same could be said of the referee. Anderson might well have had a Uefa Cup medal to go with his two European Cup ones had it not been for the grubby dealings of the Spaniard Guruceta Muro, whose ridiculously biased decisions were later explained by the fact that he had picked up an £18,000 bribe from the Belgians.

# DEEP INTO THE FOREST

Forest could hardly have come off worse if Manuel from *Fawlty Towers* had been in charge. Assisted by a preposterous penalty against Kenny Swain, who had apparently sneezed dangerously, and with a last-minute Paul Hart header ruled out for no apparent reason other than that Muro did not like his perm, Anderlecht won 3-0 in Brussels to overturn a 2-0 deficit from the first leg. Hart's 'goal' would have seen Forest through on the away-goal rule.

The true story only emerged years later when a gang of Belgian blackmailers was arrested, having allegedly found out about the bung and been paid hundreds of thousands of pounds not to turn Anderlecht over to the authorities.

Anderson winces as he recalls the sense of bitter injustice. He was one of the lucky ones - after all, he already had an impressive haul of medals. But it felt like scant consolation at the time, as did the year-long ban that Uefa dished out to Anderlecht.

"What I really remember is that after the match we weren't allowed to take the tape with us," says Anderson. "We were so incensed about what had happened we wanted to get hold of the video, bring it back to England and show everybody, including Uefa.

"Then we found out a few years later the referee had been bought. Unbelievable. Usually, Cloughie's teams were brought up that if the referee makes a bad decision you just get on with it. But there were a couple of decisions that night that were too strange to be an accident. It was criminal what happened that night.

"We wanted compensation, and we deserved it. Think about what we missed out on. If we'd gone on to win the cup there would have been a monetary gain, not to mention winning another medal.

"It went to the Belgian courts and the idea was to highlight what had happened while Euro 2000 was being played in Belgium, but for whatever reason the legal thing just petered out in the end."

I had been told to expect Anderson to be unsentimental but that is not how he comes across. Before heading back to the table where Whiteside is waiting, he talks of his fondness for Nottingham, and Clifton in particular, speaking proudly about some of the other footballers, Darren Huckerby and Jermaine Jenas among them, who have grown up on the same estate. Anderson now lives in Altrincham where he runs a business that organises pro-am golf tournaments. "I need to get back to Nottingham more often," he concludes.

He also expresses his regret about the wholesale changes that saw the break-up of the European Cup-winning teams. "You never know, maybe we could have won some more trophies if we had stayed together," he ponders. "Maybe it was the money side of it - people realising they could get more at other clubs. Whatever the reason, it suddenly fell apart and I was one of the last ones there."

Anderson clearly missed his mates - Garry Birtles, who funnily enough never took to the nickname Hitler so was known as Charlie Chaplin; Martin 'The Squire' O'Neill, who used to laugh "like a leaking gas cylinder you couldn't shut off"; John McGovern who was considered the "gentleman of the team" because of his culinary tastes; Tony Woodcock who "was so quiet you sometimes had to shake him to make sure he was awake" and the bookworm John Robertson who would "read anything from *Playboy* to *The Rise and Fall of the Roman Empire*."

How would they have described him? O'Neill, for one, has hailed Anderson as the best right-back he has ever played with or against, and there are few better judges of a player than the Irishman. In later years at Manchester United Sir Alex Ferguson remembers a player whose "resolute professionalism at right-back and bubbly, contagious enthusiasm in the dressing-room were worth a lot more than the £250,000 we paid Arsenal."

Frank Clark remembers Anderson being "too good and too mean" to give anything away and, to a man, his old teammates will argue that he deserved far more than 30 international caps.

As David Miller, of the *Daily Express*, put it after the European Cup defeat of Liverpool in 1978: "Forest's eclipse of the champions was accomplished with the defensive efficiency that has been the hallmark of Liverpool themselves. And none was more efficient than Anderson. He can develop into an attacking full-back comparable to the memorable Djalmar Santos of Brazil's World Cup-winning team. The timing of his tackling and interceptions is now as clean and sharp as any defender in the First Division, reminding one in certain moments even of Bobby Moore."

# DEEP INTO THE FOREST

There is not much higher praise than that, but in one respect Anderson should be remembered as doing more for the national game than the man who lifted the Jules Rimet trophy in 1966. Anderson did not single-handedly banish racism from the game, nor did he try to. But he did advance the cause of enlightenment through his skill, courage and dignity. He turned the volume down on the bigots and for that alone he deserves considerable respect.

# SEVEN

# Kenny Burns

*It was Peter Taylor's idea. 'Forget it,' I said. 'I
don't want trouble-makers, I don't want shithouses, and I don't
want an ugly bastard like Kenny Burns littering my club.'*

**Brian Clough**

POOR KEVIN KEEGAN. At the best of times Kenny Burns could look like a cross between a scarecrow and Shane McGowan from the Pogues, but even by his standards of aesthetic awfulness there was something particularly gruesome about him on that balmy Madrid evening. It was May 28th, 1980, the European Cup final against Hamburg, and as the two sets of players lined up in the tunnel of the Bernabeu Keegan glanced over at the man whose ferocious brand of old-school, blood-and-thunder defending stood between him and the Continent's most cherished football prize. Bad move. At precisely that moment Burns was in the process of yanking out his false teeth for a hard night's graft. He looked sweaty, agitated and, quite frankly, a little bit mad. And when he saw Keegan, the gap-toothed Glaswegian bared his gums and met his opponent's gaze with the most terrifying grimace he could muster. For a split second Keegan must have felt as though he had won the lottery only for his ticket to go through the wash. "You're a dead man," Larry Lloyd whispered in his ear.

Time, they say, is a great healer and Keegan has needed a quarter of a century to get over his disappointment that night. "Magnificent" is the word he uses to describe Burns's performance - but it is through gritted teeth.

He describes the John Robertson strike that beat Rudi Kargus in the Hamburg goal as a "poor shot" and a "soft goal to concede." It

93

turns out he refused to visit the winners' traditional post-match banquet. "I'm a bad loser and I was gutted," he explains. "Neither was I a lover of Nottingham Forest."

When I regale Burns with Keegan's version of events he affords himself a smile of satisfaction. He is sunburnt, has just played a "shite" round of golf at Oakmere Park in Oxton and is in no mood to offer any apologies. "I had to take my teeth out at some point," he laughs. "But I'd have thought Keegan would have known exactly what he was going to get between myself and Lloydie anyway. He was a good player, Kevin. He worked hard, he was busy and he scored goals. It was important Larry and me stopped him and to do that we may have had to use - how can I put it? - a bit of intimidation and one or two over-the-top tackles. But tough on him.

"I remember getting a lovely 50-50 with him on the touchline, right by the halfway line. All credit to him, he put his heart and soul into it, too. He went in hard but I went in harder. I don't think Kevin was up for it after that. Seriously, I get the impression he was thinking: 'Christ, I don't want any more of this . . .'

"It was bread-and-butter stuff for me but as the game went on Kevin kept going a wee bit further and further into defence, which was great for me. Poor bloke, he was near the halfway line by the time the game ended."

The first thing to understand about Burns is that he was more than just a kicker. Much more. Sure, he had a temper that could set off a car alarm. Without doubt, there are a few horror stories to be told about that broken nose. He could send an Alsatian scampering for cover with one snarl and there will be a few retired centre-forwards who still bear the scars of his X-rated challenges, when he tackled like a runaway threshing machine. But he could play, too. He was courageous in the tackle, dominant in the air, read the play brilliantly and when required he could also bring the ball forward and spray it around. Peter Taylor described him as "the Scottish Bobby Moore - only with more skill."

Taught at an early age "you don't have studs in your arse," Burns preferred to stay on his feet rather than dive in - most of the time, anyway.

# KENNY BURNS

Forest's fans voted him their player-of-the-year in 1978 and 1981 and even if the nation's sports journalists might not always have given Clough's teams as much credit as they deserved, the Football Writers' Association got it spot on when they named him their footballer-of-the-year in the championship-winning season. He is the only Forest player ever to win it, even if Nigel Jemson reckons he should have had it one year.

"Lloydie and me had one of the best understandings you could ever have in a central defensive partnership," says Burns. "You can go through all the great pairings - Colin Todd and Roy McFarland, Jack Charlton and Norman Hunter, Mark Lawrenson and Alan Hansen - and I regard us as being up there with the very, very best. We knew how to play, how to cover, how to tackle and if anyone wanted to rough it up a wee bit, well that was no problem either.

"We tried to do things within the rules, of course, but sometimes you had to break one here and there, especially if you could get away with it. My style was simple: I used to kick someone, apologise to the ref and say it wouldn't happen again. Then I'd pick up the player and as I did so I'd tell him: 'I'm gonna kick you again the next time too, son.'

"If someone came in with elbows, they'd get elbows back. And they'd be guaranteed to get it. I liked to put my authority on a player, just to let them know I wasn't going to take any shit off them. That way, they knew what they were going to get right away. And if I got half a chance I'd go through someone. That was the way it was in those days. It was about getting your retaliation in first."

Clough certainly grew fond of the old warrior, admittedly after a difficult start. He even asked Burns, or 'Kenneth' as he insisted on calling him (much to the embarrassment of the Glasgow tearaway), to captain the side when John McGovern suffered a groin injury before the replayed 1978 League Cup final against Liverpool at Old Trafford. Burns therefore has the distinction of being the first Forest player to lift a trophy (excluding the Anglo Scottish Cup) during Clough's reign.

Not bad considering that Clough was so opposed to the idea of signing him when Peter Taylor first suggested it that it caused serious friction between the management pair. Burns had committed a tackle on Aston Villa's Gary Robson that made its way into a *Times* feature in 2004 about the 50 worst-ever tackles and even Birmingham's chairman David Wiseman had warned Clough: "Don't buy him - he's trouble."

Clough worked himself into a froth of moral indignation but Taylor promised that if Burns messed up he would take the blame. And it has gone down in folklore how Taylor did some undercover work to see whether Burns was the untamed, drinking, gambling, pub-brawler that he had read about.

"I like a flutter - the horses, the dogs, whatever - and I used to go to Perry Barr for a few £5 bets with Paul Hendrie," says Burns.

"Apparently Pete Taylor was watching our every move from the shadows. He'd followed us to the track and put his collar up, as well as wearing some dark glasses and a flat cap, so nobody would spot him."

Burns did not recognise Taylor in his disguise and nor did he realise that the punter so often at his shoulder as he placed a bet was Forest's chief scout Maurice Edwards.

"They didn't see anything they didn't like. It wasn't true, for starters, that I was in a stolen car. I had an old Vauxhall Viva back then and there was a lot of stuff flying about, that it was stolen and had no road tax etc.

"They thought they were getting a bad boy but I knew Brian Clough was getting a good signing. He phoned me and I went to meet him on a Friday night at a pub near Tamworth called the Four Counties. We had a couple of wee drinks and talked about money. Then the next day he invited me and my then girlfriend to Bardills garden centre at Long Eaton. It turned out there was a sweet pea exhibition and they were naming some flowers after him.

"I didn't have a clue. I thought we were going to look at some peas - garden peas, that is. I mean, peas are peas, aren't they? Green things. What kind of peas are sweet peas? In Scotland, flowers are just things whose heads you kick off when you've had a few pints on a Saturday night."

The horticultural lesson over, an even bigger surprise was waiting for Burns, then 23, when Clough decided that the man who

**Stuart Pearce and Nigel Clough show how much
Forest mean to them, celebrating a Psycho special
at Manchester City in 1992.**

Neil Webb was the 1,000th player to win an England cap.

Roy Keane in his debut season at the City Ground.
At £47,000 he represents one of the club's
greatest pieces of business.

**Trevor Francis with the European Cup.
His header against Malmo justified every last penny
of his £1million price tag.**

**Garry Birtles, the local lad, shoots down Southampton
in the 1979 League Cup final.**

**A six-year-old Nigel Clough picks up some tips
from his father in the Brighton dug-out . . .**

**. . . and 18 years later as the core of the side that reached
Wembley six times in four seasons.**

**Kenny Burns shows how many European Cup winner's medals he has won.**

**Viv Anderson made history as the first black player to win an England cap.**

Archie Gemmill, a little man with a big talent. As player (left)...

...and as coach (right) "The best of the lot," said Brian Clough.

You'll never beat Des Walker. Forest's brilliant centre-half
keeps on top of Manchester United's Mark Hughes.

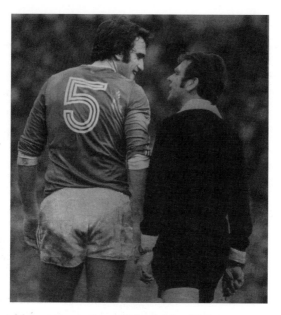

**Honest, it wasn't me. Larry Lloyd tries his best to sweet-talk Pat Partridge in the 1978 League Cup final against Liverpool.**

**John Robertson was so good Liverpool used to stick two defenders on him - and it still never worked.**

**Roy Keane and Steve Chettle congratulate Stuart Pearce
after he opens the scoring in the 1991 FA Cup final - but
Spurs had the last laugh.**

**Kenny Burns, David Needham and Garry Birtles arrive
at East Midlands Airport after Forest had conquered
Europe for a second time.**

**Life wasn't always so sweet for Garry Birtles - check out his expression on the bench beside Brian Clough, Peter Taylor and Jimmy Gordon.**

**Des Walker's departure for Sampdoria can be brought out as Exhibit A in the club's relegation in 1993. Here he takes on Nigel Clough in the Makita tournament.**

John Robertson shows off the 1979 League Cup at Wembley,
closely followed by Garry Birtles, John McGovern
and Martin O'Neill.

Viv Anderson was nicknamed Spider
because of his telescopic legs.

Ian Storey-Moore, Forest's George Best, used to attract
opposition defenders like moths to a lightbulb.

The fearsome Kenny Burns demonstrates why he
was regarded as one of the most formidable
centre-halves of his generation.

**Only Franz Beckenbauer has lifted the European Cup more times than John McGovern.**

**The man who made it all possible, Brian Clough.**
**As the banner said: "Heaven XI just got a new manager."**

had built a reputation as a marauding centre-forward at Birmingham City, scoring 20 goals alongside Trevor Francis the previous season, would be taking Sammy Chapman's place at centre-half.

First, though, Clough wanted to show his £150,000 signing he had a talent for getting his retaliation in first, too. Showing the wrecking-ball subtlety for which he was famed, Clough's welcome-to-Forest speech included the description of Burns as a "bloody tramp" as well as telling him he was "in the gutter" and lucky not to be arrested driving such a clapped-out car. The scruffy Scotsman did himself no favours when it transpired he had associated sweet peas with the type he usually had with his sausages and chips.

"Get shaved and get yourself a decent coat," Clough told him. Not that Burns resented it. Quite the opposite. "Brian Clough was a manager I could relate to - a players' man. He put me on the straight and narrow and was like an adopted father. But anyone could relate to him. When he was on television or writing in the papers people from all walks of life would take notice.

"He told you straight. If he thought you were shit, you were shit. And if he thought you were great, you were great. Simplicity. We wouldn't even have team talks. He'd just saunter into the dressing room at ten to three, sit between me and Lloydie and blow his cigar smoke on him, just to wind him up. But his word was always final and when he spoke everyone listened.

"I went into his office one day to ask for a day off because I was getting married. His eyes lit up. 'Tell you what - I'll come along,' he said. He brought his wife with him . . . and his gardener. But I didn't mind. To me, he will always be the number one manager in football. Ever."

Did Clough tame him? "He made a big impression on me but I wouldn't say he tamed me. The difference was that at Birmingham I used to get a lot of bookings for dissent. I was a striker and I reckoned I could beat anyone in the air. So if the crosses were coming in where I wanted them, everything would be fine. But if the balls were not going in I'd start to get a wee bit angry. If the ref gave something against me, I might give him a bit of verbal out of frustration. But if you did that under Cloughie there'd be a fine waiting for you. He would come down on you like a ton of bricks if you were booked for dissent."

Clough even invited Clive Thomas into his office to congratulate him for booking Burns in one match. Most referees would dread a summons to a manager's inner sanctum, but Clough simply told him: "Well done - you keep doing that."

Burns looks back on those moments with a sheepish smile. Another time Clough fined him for nearly giving away a goal playing a casual pass across his own penalty area. "It was against Manchester City. But, hey, no problem - I'd done wrong so I paid the penalty and accepted it. I'd tried to find John Robertson across the other side of the penalty area but Dennis Tueart got a little touch on it and it went out for a goal-kick.

"At half-time the Gaffer told Liam O'Kane to get the fine sorted so I came in at full time and waiting for me was the white envelope with the red tree on the front. I had a few of those envelopes in my time but I knew Clough wouldn't tolerate me getting booked for dissent so I cut it out. I came to Forest and in that first year I didn't miss a game through suspension."

He did, however, have the occasional bust-up with Clough, not least when television cameras caught him head-butting Arsenal's Richie Powling during a 3-0 defeat at Highbury in September 1978 - only his fifth league game for the club and Forest's first defeat in the title-winning season.

Presumably with his fingers crossed behind his back, Burns claimed he had done nothing more than sneeze, but it was a vapid excuse. With the chin-up, drawling, nasal sneer that was forever Clough, the Forest manager fined him and condemned him in the newspapers: "He can play the rest of the season for nothing or he can become one of the best and highest-paid players in the game. It's up to him."

Burns learned his lesson and repaid the faith that was shown in him, not just from Clough but Taylor too. It was Taylor, after all, who had gambled most on a hothead whose reputation had frightened off most other managers. "It was like good-cop bad-cop with them, but they were brilliant together," says Burns. "It was like gin and tonic - they just went."

# KENNY BURNS

Clough's outstanding memory of his No 6 was his flattening of Kenny Dalglish with a typically industrial challenge during the European Cup tie at Liverpool in 1978. As the pair of them got to their feet Burns fixed his most impenetrable stare on his fellow Scot and, in a moment of chilling menace, slowly pointed his finger in Dalglish's face.

It was reminiscent of that famous picture of Dave Mackay, jutting jaw, barrel chest, indomitable spirit, taking umbrage with a terrified Billy Bremner - only Burns had the temerity to do it to the talisman of Anfield directly in front of the Kop. No words needed to be said - Burns had kept his finger there long enough for the message to be clear.

In that split second Clough swore blind he saw the blood drain from Dalglish's face and, sure enough, the most penetrative forward of his generation scarcely touched the ball again. Dalglish cannot have relished his games against Forest - another time Lloyd careered into him with such recklessness it wrenched off both his boots.

"Teams would come to our place and Larry would sort out one striker and Kenny would sort the other out," Ian Bowyer said once. "With Kenny there was a thin line between what was fair and what was unfair. But after ten minutes the opposition strikers would be looking over their shoulders. His first year was the best. He was made footballer-of-the-year. Can you believe it? A rogue like Kenny Burns alongside gentleman of the game such as Stanley Matthews and Tom Finney. It's incredible."

Burns identifies the destruction of Keegan's attacking talents in Madrid as his most memorable achievement in the Garibaldi red. Under strict orders, Forest's players had deliberately cold-shouldered Keegan that night. Clough did not need to have scrutinised Forest's opponents to understand that Keegan was their most potent attacker and there was nobody wishing the European footballer-of-the-year best wishes in the tunnel or arranging to have a drink after the match. In fact, there was not even a nod of recognition.

The idea was to let Keegan know it would be a difficult night before a ball had even been kicked in anger and then Burns, the man who put 'stop' into stopper, would handle him once the match was underway.

# DEEP INTO THE FOREST

"I don't want to mention this," Larry Lloyd whispered in Keegan's ear. "But Kenny isn't feeling very friendly towards you today."

"It's not going to be like that, is it?" replied Keegan.

"Sorry mate, he's out to do your legs, Burnsy's gonna do you."

The master plan worked perfectly. In fact, Keegan was reduced to such anonymity Burns should have taken his opponent's jersey as a souvenir, much as the tribesmen of the Danekil in the Horn of Africa sport on a necklace the withered penises of the men they have killed in battle.

"That was the game that sticks out for me. The first final against Malmo, I have to say I was terrible. Big Larry carried me that night. It's funny because it had never bothered me before who I was playing against - whether it was Liverpool, England, Brazil. Bring them all on, I'd say. But I had a bad game, a horrible game, against Malmo and I can remember the Gaffer saying to me afterwards that for some reason he hadn't felt right with me from the start.

"Against Hamburg I was full of it like normal. I enjoyed that far, far better. Keegan was playing up front but we never spoke to him beforehand. The truth is we never spoke to the opposition in the tunnel, even if they were your mates. The Gaffer didn't like us being friendly.

"He'd say: 'You might have to go out there and kick them. Talk to them after the game, after you've kicked them and won the game. Have a beer with them afterwards, by all means, but not in the tunnel, during the warm-up, anything like that.'

"So, to a man, we ignored Keegan. And then Lloydie and me had to do a job on him. Like I say, to do that we might have used some over-the-top tackles, but so what? We had to stop him scoring because if he got a goal we're not winning the European Cup, and those type of matches don't come round that often."

The critics were unimpressed with Forest's conservatism, particularly after John Robertson's goal had put them ahead. In Germany it was denounced as "Blitzkrieg" football while the impartial Spanish writers branded it "soulless." Even the *Sunday Times* accused Clough of "tactical cowardice," with Garry Birtles deployed as a lone striker.

As for Keegan, he shook his head forlornly at the final whistle. "Forest are uncanny in the way they make you play to their strengths. They block off the middle with so many players and force you to go wide. Then they have two central defenders and a goalkeeper who are outstanding at dealing with crosses."

"I really couldn't give a damn what anybody else thinks about that night," says Burns. "It's our name in the record books and, for me, it was one of the greatest defensive displays of all time.

"The fact is that some of these so-called experts were reluctant to give Forest the slightest bit of credit for anything. We were too unfashionable for them and too damn good. Just look at the 42-match unbeaten league run - if that had been Manchester United or Arsenal you would have heard about it every day since."

It was a close-run thing whether the 1980 European final was Burns's greatest individual display or, as many people believe, it was actually the semi-final second leg in Cologne the previous season. The pressure on Forest had been immense after the first leg on a City Ground mudbath had ended with Yasukiho Okudera, the one-time Japanese footballer-of-the-year, scoring Cologne's equaliser in a 3-3 thriller that inspired the unforgettable headline "Japanese Sub Sinks Forest" in the *Guardian* the next morning.

Bookmakers were offering 4-1 against a Forest win in the imposing Mungersdorf stadium and, showing the sort of arrogance that fuelled Clough's dislike of Germans, Cologne had already decided their place in the final was such a foregone conclusion that they had arranged their supporters' buses and printed their tickets.

To the particular irritation of the Forest players, Cologne's formidable international striker Dietmer Muller even boasted to the German press about how easily the Bundesliga champions would go through. But with 6,000 Forest fans having made their way to Germany, Burns *et al* had different ideas.

"I remember they'd booked their hotel for the final and they'd even invited one of their ex-players over to it. It came out in the press to stir things up but I wasn't that bothered, if I'm being honest. We knew the game wasn't over and that we could go anywhere and win.

"I've never seen anyone as confident, for example, as Pete Taylor was before that game. He was absolutely adamant we would win. He had been over to see them and he was so confident. 'We'll beat these," he told us. I'm sure he had a good bet on us, too, because he liked a little flutter. We kept them out - Nottingham Forest were built on clean sheets - and then second half, we get a corner, Ian Bowyer heads it in, 1-0 to us and we're in the European Cup final. Fantastic."

As for the outspoken Muller, he did not even last until half-time. Between them, Burns and Lloyd had made it a mission of theirs to identify the striker for, let's say, some preferential treatment.

"The team spirit at that time was just incredible," says Burns. "We used to go everywhere together. Every Wednesday was golf day. We had a few - Martin O'Neill, John Robertson, Viv Anderson and Tony Woodcock - who didn't play but you could guarantee they'd come up afterwards for a beer and a sandwich. And every Friday we'd walk up to the little café [McKay's] on Radcliffe Road, get the cobs in, drink cups of tea and sit there talking football.

"It reached the point where everyone knew what every player was thinking. That spirit of togetherness was Nottingham Forest and on the field we would do anything for the manager. He kept everything straightforward with us. We did nothing fancy-dan because his philosophy was simple - keep it on the floor, knock it around and if you've got the ball they can't score."

After four highly successful seasons under Clough's tuition, incorporating a league championship medal, two European Cups, one Super Cup and two League Cups, Burns moved to Leeds United for £400,000 as part of the mass exodus of players that saw a great Forest team disbanded with reckless haste.

Most observers would have thought a team of bullying bruisers such as Leeds would have been ideal for him, but he struggled to get anywhere close to the exhilarating peaks he had reached on Trentside.

In Eddie Gray's autobiography, *Marching on Together*, he remembers: "He [Burns] did okay, but without Brian Clough and in a set-up that was less regimented and disciplined than the one he had come from, he did not look the same player."

Forest's fans might also be intrigued to learn that, rather than making enemies of his opponents, his biggest fall-out at Leeds was with a certain young centre-half by the name of Paul Hart. Indeed, the friction was so bad between them that one of the first things Gray did when he took over from Allan Clarke as manager in 1982 was to get the pair of them into his office for a clear-the-air meeting.

Since ending his professional career Burns has gone through the ex-footballer's cliché of running a pub, been the scourge of non-league centre-forwards with Grantham Town (under Martin O'Neill's management) and Ilkeston Town, as well as working for a giftware company and as a salesman in the caravan business, based in Uttoxeter.

His home now is Derby, but being an ex-Forest player in the wrong town cannot be too much of a problem when you look as scary as he does. He has lost the straw-yellow mane, but living in the Midlands for 30 years has not diluted the thick Glaswegian accent and, though you would never tell him to his face, his bald pate, burly frame and slightly frightening glare give him the look of someone who could be working on the door of the Trent Bridge Inn.

It is easy to sympathise with O'Neill, for example, when just before a friendly against the Austrian champions Wacker Innsbruck Burns jogged over with his false teeth wrapped in tissue and asked him to look after them. O'Neill was a substitute and, though his first reaction is not a matter of public record, it is fair to say his expression was that of a man who had just found a pubic hair in his coleslaw.

Imagine the Irishman's horror when he jumped up to celebrate a Forest goal and realised not only that the dentures had fallen out of his tracksuit pocket, but that in his enthusiasm he had just jumped on top of them, smashing them into several pieces. A rookie gladiator going into the Colosseum, unarmed and wearing nothing more than a loincloth, might not have felt as apprehensive as O'Neill did when he had to break the news to his toothless colleague.

Likewise, Milton Veira of AEK Athens picked on the wrong man when he was foolish enough to land a left hook on Burns during the European Cup second-round tie in 1978 at the primitive

# DEEP INTO THE FOREST

Philadelphia stadium in Athens. Goodness knows what Burns would have done to him if the referee had not got there first, showing the Uruguayan striker a red card. It would not have been a pretty sight.

Eighteen years after the Malmo game the Forest players had a reunion dinner and O'Neill, almost as skilled an exponent of the put-down as Clough himself, went for a belated form of revenge when he was asked to name the teammate he regarded as the best footballer. "I don't know about the best, but I know who was the ugliest," he said, turning towards Burns. "They couldn't show the Forest highlights on television before 9p.m." Taking it all in his stride, Burns rose to his feet and politely asked O'Neill how many times he had won the footballer-of-the-year award.

Beneath the "stitch-that" exterior, Burns is certainly engaging company. Okay, he sometimes comes across as being the kid at school who would bring in a magnifying glass to burn insects. But Taylor used to describe Burns as being a "pussy cat really" and even Clough sometimes reminisced about "a charming man". Ask any member of that Forest team and they can all see a lovable side in Burns. He never bore a grudge, he could take the dressing-room ribbing and his enthusiasm was contagious.

"Kenny was an intimidating guy but he could play as well," says Frank Clark, his old defensive colleague. "A lot of people made the mistake of underestimating him, but he was footballer-of-the-year in 1978 and you don't get an award like that just from kicking people.

"Don't get me wrong, he was a formidable character. In the modern game he would never have been allowed to get away with some of the things he did back then. But I have to say that his reputation was overplayed a bit. He was never as bad as he was painted. He was a top player, as simple as that. Between him and Larry Lloyd they formed a formidable barrier. You would do well to get through them - although if you saw the size of them today you'd do even better to get round them!

"Coming to Forest certainly helped him. Having a manager like Brian Clough helped for starters, the other players were a strong and sobering influence, and he benefited from getting married, too.

I can't remember any incidents of him losing his temper, or anything like that."

"The first time I met Kenny after he'd gone to Forest I couldn't believe it was the same person," recalls Don Dorman, the Birmingham City scout who had brought Burns south of the border after three sending-offs in four youth matches blew his chances of becoming a Glasgow Rangers player. "In the old days he was like a lad who had just come out of Borstal. But I'd never witnessed such a change in someone as when he came up to my office a month or so after he'd gone to Forest and asked: 'Can I come in Mr Dorman?' I was absolutely shocked. And he conducted himself so well . . ."

A quarter of a century later, Burns is just as passionate as he ever was, as you can probably tell from his unashamedly biased input on local radio. "It's hard at times," he laments. "Sometimes you just want to say 'that player's shit' . . . but you can't.

"It's simple, really. I love Forest. You can't be associated with a club as great as this for as long as I have without a true bond being built up."

Has he mellowed with age? Probably. But there is still a side of Kenneth Burns that it would not be wise to upset. Take this story from the first leg of the play-off semi-final against Sheffield United in 2003: "I was down in the tunnel at half-time and Robert Page is having a go at Darren Huckerby. So I step in between them to tell them both to forget it. I'm saying: 'Leave it, you can do it out on the pitch.' But Page is carrying a bottle of water and as he turns away, he walked about four or five yards and then sprayed some of it over me."

An annoying squirt from an annoying squirt. "I just went for him. I couldn't get to him because there were so many people in the way, but I flew for him good and proper. Then we had Neil Warnock [the Sheffield United manager], the arse that he is, complaining that there were 'ex-players who wanted to make a name for themselves.' I've got no respect for that guy. Absolute arse. It was something out of nothing for me. But he was lucky he got away when he did."

# EIGHT

# Larry Lloyd

*He was always troubled by a back injury but it was
less of a problem than his big mouth.*

**Peter Taylor**

A WORD OF ADVICE for David Platt: don't go to Marbella on your holidays. "I'd love to bump into the little slimebag," says a tanned Larry Lloyd, still wearing a T-shirt and shorts even though it is winter, and clearly enjoying his new life on the Spanish resort. "I owe Platt," he says darkly. "What goes around comes around. And he'll have his day, believe me."

Lloyd is only too happy to clarify the reasons for his malevolence. "I blame Platt for Century radio giving me the boot," he says. "I used to love that job, doing the phone-in and commentating on matches. But Platt was fed up of hearing me slaughter him. He told them he'd have nothing to do with the radio station as long as I was working for them. I hate the man - absolutely hate him."

Platt will have to convince himself that Lloyd means it when he declares he "will never come back to live in England." Otherwise the ex-Forest manager might spend the rest of his life looking over his shoulder. Lloyd, after all, is the sort of man a Rottweiler would think twice about biting - a broken-nosed, barn-door of a defender from the days when Brian Clough and Peter Taylor rivalled the strictest hospital matron in their belief in the sanctity of clean sheets.

This is a man who lifted Peter Shilton up by his throat during one dressing-room argument and, along with Kenny Burns, took professional pride in forming the ugliest, meanest, most fearsome central defensive partnership in the country.

# LARRY LLOYD

If Burns had a face like a clenched fist, Lloyd was 6ft 3ins of Frankenstein-esque menace. His language could make Billy Connolly blush, his handshake could crush a conker and, after two decades out of the game, his elephantine girth gives him the appearance of an inflatable WWF wrestler. The nutcase who comes out wearing a black mask and a skull-and-crossbones cape, breaks every rule going and ends up throwing the promoter over the ropes.

"I listen to the idiots on television going on about these so-called hard guys in the Premiership and it pisses me off, to be honest. Robbie Savage? Are you having a laugh? He would have been a fairy in our day. A total nancy-boy. Even Vinnie Jones - he would have been killed. There would have been people queuing up to take him out here [he points at his Adam's apple]. Poor Vinnie would have been murdered."

Lloyd is not the sort of guy it is wise to offend. Nor, with all due respect, is he a man to get stuck on a see-saw with. Yet his huge, slightly intimidating frame should not betray the fact that he is one of the more approachable ex-Forest stars. Ever since I tracked down his Spanish mobile number and invited myself over he could hardly have been more obliging, and it soon becomes apparent why he harbours such a grudge against Platt. Lloyd, quite simply, is never happier than when he is going through his old Forest anecdotes. At times he can hardly get to the punchline as he wheezes with laughter, slaps his thigh and wipes his eyes. Losing his job at Century was one thing, but his real grievance was that it severed his ties with a club he loves.

Lloyd won three England caps and a championship medal in the early-70s at Liverpool but when Clough and Taylor gambled on the burly, brash Bristolian he was drifting out of favour in a Coventry side that finished the 1976/77 season only a point above the First Division relegation places.

"Initially it was on a month's loan and I went straight into the side at Sammy Chapman's expense. Bloody hell, that didn't go down well. Sammy hated me being at Forest and he didn't mind if I knew about it. He didn't want me there and was ice cool with me.

# DEEP INTO THE FOREST

"The fans took his side. Sammy was clearly their hero and suddenly this big old geezer Larry Lloyd has taken his place. My debut was at Hull, a 1-0 defeat, and the away fans used to be tucked away in the corner at Boothferry Park. All the way through the game I was getting booed and hearing 'Oh Sammy, Sammy . . .'

"I didn't have a bad game and Cloughie came in afterwards and asked me to sign permanently. He even had the forms in his briefcase but I wanted to wait until the month was up. I was a bit reluctant because I was established in the First Division and Forest were 12th in the Second Division. I didn't really know much about Cloughie except he was that mouthy sod off television. I was only 27 and I thought: 'Bloody hell, am I ready to drop down yet?'

"I went back to Gordon Milne at Coventry and he made it clear he no longer wanted me. They were in dire financial straits and couldn't afford my wages any longer. In fact, things were so tight at Coventry we were under orders to switch the lights off in every room to save electricity. Plus I'd been slagging everyone off there. So I took the chance and, fuck me, what a great decision it turned out."

Lloyd signed for £60,000 and within four months had served his first suspension for going over 20 disciplinary points. Clough promptly dropped him for a match against Hereford United and threatened to sell him. "Lloyd has to be taught a lesson, even if it damages our chances of promotion," he said. "Whether I'm manager of England, Forest or Nottingham Pork Butchers I am determined to preserve my standards of team behaviour and discipline."

Lloyd eventually offered to pay a fine if it meant returning to the team and, presumably with a heavy sigh, agreed not to commit any more premeditated acts of violence. Well, to cut them down anyway. Once Clough bought Kenny Burns from Birmingham City there were times when the two centre-halves seemed to be trying to outdo each other in terms of being regarded as the team's hard man.

"I'd played against Kenny before when he was at Birmingham and - surprise, surprise - we'd had a few tussles. Then he was suddenly playing next to me and, by Christ, I found out what a good player he was. For the next four years we just gelled. We were

108

widely considered the best central defensive partnership in the country and strikers hated facing us.

"Cloughie never gave us specific instructions to take someone out. He was clever and he didn't want us telling the press: 'Well, the Gaffer said to break his legs.' But we knew what he wanted. He'd point his finger at us and say: 'Kenneth, Bighead, you know what to do' and then he'd walk away.

"We hunted in twos. I'd take the big guy because I was tallest and Kenny would take the smaller guy because he was a bit sharper on the deck. Then we'd make our own little rules. Back then you got a suspension if you reached 20 disciplinary points so if we had a fight on our hands we'd have a quick chat on the pitch. 'How many points are you on, Ken?'

'I'm on 18 - what about you?'

'I'm only on 14 - I'll take him out first.'

"Honestly, you could get away with so much more then. It didn't matter who it was. I would give Kenny Dalglish a couple of yards so he could turn and then hammer him. Sorry, *tackle him*.

"A few years after I stopped playing I saw Kenny in the bar at Anfield. He came over, shook my hand and said: 'Thank fuck, you're out of the First Division now.' I took that as just about the greatest compliment I have ever had."

There were times when Lloyd, by his own admission, overstepped the mark, such as Southampton's visit to the City Ground in February 1977, when the fog was so bad the game had to be abandoned after 47 minutes.

Lloyd had an old grudge against Peter Osgood. "He was naughty, Ossie. He was always trying to break my legs. The fog was coming over the Trent End and the referee was at the far end. I thought: 'Come on you bastard, over here.' He trotted over. Whoosh! Landed him one with my nut.

"He had a go at me: 'Fucking hell, what's going on?'

"I shouted: 'That's for all the years I was at Liverpool and you were at Chelsea trying to break my leg.' The referee missed it. Half the crowd did too. But guess who saw it? That bastard Cloughie. It cost me a week's wages, that one."

# DEEP INTO THE FOREST

His fallouts with Clough, and to a lesser degree Taylor, became a standard way of life at Forest. "Larry Lloyd was murder for the first few months," Taylor once said. "All my contacts advised me not to sign him. My friends said: 'You're crackers. This fellow is the big "I am" - he's full of himself and no one can tell him anything.'

"I told them: 'On the other hand he's big, he can head the ball, he's an international, he's tough and, besides, I like arrogant players. If he gets too cocky Brian and I will sort him out.'

"Well, I have to confess he needed more than the average sorting-out - he seemed to imagine he was dealing with a pair of non-league managers. Interruptions from players were forbidden when either Brian or myself were speaking, but Lloyd cut in continually. He thought he had the right to say what he liked when he liked.

"I told him: 'You want to keep your mouth shut because we're the best thing that ever happened to you.' I kept hammering away at Lloyd with the example of Roy McFarland as a player, as a person and as a perfect professional. But it was almost a year before he knuckled down."

Even then, there were times when Lloyd stretched their patience close to breaking point. Like the time Tampa Bay Rowdies visited the City Ground for a friendly in October 1980.

"I didn't have the mind for a friendly game," says Lloyd. "I was always shit or bust, you know, and I just couldn't take it seriously. There were people with pompons coming down in parachutes. What a load of garbage!

"The ball was played to me four minutes into the game and, feeling as I did, I went to back-heel it to Frank Clark and fell over. Up went the board - number five - and I was substituted four minutes into the game.

"I walked back to Clough and shouted: 'You're a fucking loony, you are.'

"And he yelled back: 'So are you - fuck off.' So I did. I went home."

Three months earlier Forest had played Toronto Blizzard on a pre-season tour of Canada. "The bigger the game the better I was," says Lloyd. "The smaller the game, I couldn't care less. So for this one I couldn't give two fucks.

"For some reason they had us walking out in two lines for the national anthems, trying to make out it was a big match. It was a boiling hot day and I had my socks down.

"They raised the maple-leaf flag and were about to play the Canadian anthem when the referee sidled over to me [he puts on a Canadian accent]: 'Heeey man, pull your socks up.'

'You what? Are you taking the piss?' I said.

[Canadian accent] 'Hey dude, show some respect for the flag, man - pull your socks up.'

'Respect for the flag? Go on, fuck off.'

"We were lined up and the referee ran over to the dug-out to have a word with Cloughie. Suddenly up goes the board again. Number five. I was being substituted before the bloody kick-off! The crowd were going mad and the boys were pissing themselves."

Bigheaded, temperamental and sensitive (all his own words), it was no surprise that Lloyd clashed so frequently with an idiosyncratic iconoclast such as Clough.

The most famous occasion came the morning after Forest's European Cup tie against AEK Athens when Lloyd reported for the flight home in a casual jacket and jeans rather than his club blazer. Clough had turned up in his customary green sweatshirt but when he saw Lloyd he went back to his hotel room and returned in his blazer, tie, shirt, flannels and polished shoes.

He then fined Lloyd who refused to pay and was dropped for the weekend match against Ipswich. Lloyd stormed into the ground on the Monday morning brandishing a transfer request, but Clough had gone on holiday. By the time he returned, Lloyd had cooled down and decided to pay up.

"I used to get more fines than anyone," he says proudly. "Burnsy, despite being a bit of a rebel, generally went with the flow. There was Martin O'Neill who always answered back but he was a little bit different because he used long words. He was academically brighter than Cloughie and had been to university, so he used words that Cloughie didn't understand. It used to piss Cloughie off, and Martin knew that.

# DEEP INTO THE FOREST

"My problem was that I was always trying to rebel. I suppose you learn as you get older. Looking back now, I realise I was never going to beat the man. Like the incident with the blazer. I was so bloody mad with him fining me I refused to pay, had a blazing row and made it even worse. It was stupid of me. I was just costing myself money and in the end I had to pay it."

It was fortunate for Lloyd that he was one of the highest-paid players at the club. "I came here on £180 a week and when the rest of the lads found out they went ape-shit. John Robertson was the worst, followed by Martin O'Neill and Viv Anderson. They were on £80 but because I had come from First Division sides I was on decent money. Oh, they went ape-shit when they found out I was nearly on twice as much as them."

He may not always have liked Clough but he certainly respected him. "You just took the abuse. All those prima donnas who said they wouldn't play for Clough - what a load of crap. You knew that come the end of the season you'd have a decent wad in the bank and a medal on the sideboard.

"I always get asked: 'Shankly or Clough?' And I always say Cloughie was the best. It was close. Shankly was a genius too. But I always say Cloughie simply because he did it with two smaller clubs, Derby and Forest, and he probably had more about him as a person. You could talk to Shanks about golf, women or television and within two minutes he would bring it back to football. With Cloughie, you could talk to him about anything from sport to politics and he would be a bloody expert on the subject.

"Shanks would always talk about the opposition, even if it was just to say Peter Lorimer was finished, or something like that. Cloughie, on the other hand, never mentioned the other team. One of his favourite sayings was: 'If we play as we can, we will beat anyone in the world'. So it would get to Friday and he would be asking: 'Who is it we're playing tomorrow?' It was inspirational.

"I can't remember ever having a tactical talk with him or a coaching lesson. 'Coaching? What's coaching?' we would say. But, as a football manager, he was second to none. He made us feel invincible. Honestly, we thought that every time we ran out we would win. We drew two consecutive home games - *drew* - against top-class opposition, and we were like: 'Fucking hell, we're losing it!'"

The tone for the Clough-Lloyd relationship was set early on when manager asked player if he liked him. "What do you mean?" Lloyd replied. "As a manager or a person?"

"Never mind about that," Clough persisted. "Do you like me?"

Lloyd thought about it for a while and then answered: "Well, as a manager I respect you more than any other man I've ever come across in the game. As a person I wouldn't stand at the bar of my local with you."

"We were both up front about it," says Lloyd, the best part of three decades later. "We didn't like each other. I thought he was a bastard, and if he were alive now he would say the same about me too.

"I would go to the other end of the bar if I saw him in a pub. Or even another pub. But some people are winners, others are losers and I knew Clough was one of the winners. And I tell you another thing - even though we didn't get on and we were always at each other's throats, every Friday when the team-sheet went up, number five was Lloyd. Every time."

The only time Lloyd feared for his place was after he broke his foot against Coventry in December 1977 and Clough immediately paid QPR £140,000 for David Needham, who had made his name as a centre-half at Notts County.

"That cheesed me right off. I was injured on the Saturday and they had another centre-half signed on the Sunday. I hobbled in on the Monday morning and hammered on Cloughie's door with my crutches. 'What the hell's going on? How do I stand?' I shouted. He took one look at my plastered-up foot and said: 'Not very well from what I can see. Now bugger off - come back to see me when you can kick a ball.'"

Needham played impeccably in the six weeks that Lloyd was sidelined. "I was watching him thinking: 'That bastard's doing far too well for my liking.' But then I got fit again, played a reserves match and we had a meeting before the next first-team match. Cloughie read out the starting XI and I was back in.

"Then he turned to Needham: 'David, you're probably wondering why I've left you out, and you're entitled to. David, you've done ever so well since I bought you. You know you've done brilliantly and I can't fault you. David, you're a lovely boy. If my daughter were looking to bring a man home to marry, you'd be that man, you're that nice I'd have you as my son-in-law.'

"Then he pointed at me. 'I hate that fucking bastard over there. And that's why you're not in the team. You're not a bastard like Larry Lloyd. And, son, I want a bastard in my defence.'

"I was ready to fly for him [he thumps the table] but then I thought: 'Hey, wait a minute, sit back down big fellow, that's a compliment'. Seriously, it might be the nicest thing he ever said to me."

Back in the team, the Lloyd-Burns alliance was an integral factor in Forest winning the league with only 24 goals conceded, equalling the best defensive record of any championship-winning side. Lloyd can also reflect with "immense pride" that the previous team to be so parsimonious was the Liverpool side of 1971, when you-know-who was in the centre of their defence.

"We had a great team spirit at Forest and that helped us," he says. "Okay, Kenny Burns and Trevor Francis had a bit of bad blood going back to their days together at Birmingham City. They weren't the best of buddies but generally they tolerated each other. I don't think Martin O'Neill liked Sammy Chapman although, come to think of it, a lot of us thought Sammy was a funny lad. But there wasn't any serious friction. If there had been I don't think we would have been as successful as we were. We played together on the pitch and we played together off the field as well."

Lloyd certainly brought his own character into the dressing room. Like the time Taylor accused him of "dozing" when Frank Stapleton headed a quick first goal in a 3-0 defeat at Highbury in September 1977. "He turned white and clenched his fists," Taylor wrote in *With Clough By Taylor*. "Everyone saw him starting to rise from his chair, positioning himself to throw a punch. I stood my ground and warned: 'If you come for me, that's you finished. You'll never kick another ball here, or anywhere else.' For once he saw sense and sat down."

Lloyd chuckles to himself as he stubs out his third cigarette in half an hour. "There were a few barneys. What I remember most of all is getting Shilts round the windpipe at half-time in one match. We were playing Dinamo Bucharest in the final of the Atletico Bilbao tournament. I'd given away a penalty in the 44th minute and their boy scored from the spot. Shilts never saved a penalty in his life, did he?

"Anyway, he came running out of his goalmouth, right up to my face, screaming it was my fault. There were 60,000 Spanish gypsies watching and I wasn't having that. We got to the dressing room and I half-throttled him. But guess what happened next? Cloughie takes me off because I'd dared to touch 'the great Shilts'.

"It was heat-of-the-moment stuff and I got on very well with Shilts otherwise. When you had him behind you it gave you a lot of confidence. The opposition striker might - just might - get past you but then they would see this bloody great gorilla bearing down on them.

"We generally gave him great protection and he was so good we knew he could get us out of a hole if we messed up. Then we had Viv Anderson on the right and he had so much pace. The amount of times a winger would think they had got past him and he would curl out that telescopic leg of his. And Frank Clark on the other side was still a top operator despite being about 102. We all knew our jobs. I wouldn't say we were the prettiest back four in the world but we were certainly the most effective."

No aficionado of defending could fail to be impressed by the manner in which a rugged old centre-half such as Lloyd could be as influential in a top-class team as any striker or star midfielder. He, like Burns, capitalised on Clough's unrivalled ability to rehabilitate and re-motivate underachievers, and Shilton is always quick to pass the credit on to his defenders when he considers his Forest record of 105 clean sheets in 272 games, with only 11 occasions when he conceded more than two in a game.

Lloyd made 214 appearances, scoring 13 times, in four-and-a-half tempestuous years at the club and his importance to the team could be accurately gauged by the impact of his absence through suspension from the 1980 League Cup final against

Wolverhampton Wanderers. Needham took his place and was involved in the mix-up with Shilton that led to Andy Gray scoring the winning goal.

Lloyd was the supporters' player-of-the-year that season and his thou-shall-not-pass, rugged, bloody-minded commitment exemplified Forest's approach to becoming two-time European champions.

"As a one-off occasion the first European Cup final against Malmo has to be the highlight," he says. "It was a shocking, horrible game, we all know that. But little Nottingham Forest, lucky to get promotion and then winning the First Division and the European Cup? We just went out there, shook everybody by the collar and told them all to fuck off.

"Kenny had a nightmare, by his own account, but I had a steady old game, heading it, stopping it, and he made a point of thanking me afterwards.

"Retaining the trophy the following year was a close second because we weren't expected to beat Hamburg, Kevin Keegan and all. They were very much the favourites, and personally that match was more pleasurable than the Malmo game because we defended so well. Without sounding bigheaded, Kenny, Shilts and myself all had the game of our lives. We just stopped everything they threw at us, so that pleases me a lot that we managed to retain it and I personally had a good game against a better side."

Lloyd had been only half-fit for the Hamburg match and Clough had put him through an unorthodox fitness test. "I'd played for England against Wales a week before, had an absolute nightmare and done my ankle ligaments," says Lloyd. "The bloody thing kept swelling up like a balloon. I should never have played in the final but I was so determined to be involved I just bit my tongue.

"On the morning of the match we had a five-a-side practice match. My ankle was strapped up and Cloughie had that look on his face. He used to get involved himself and for 20 minutes he followed me around continually kicking my ankle. If I went left, he went left: tap, tap, tap.

"He wasn't bothered about the game. He just wanted to see how sore my ankle was. I don't know how I did it, but I didn't show any pain and at the end of the session Cloughie asked me if I was fit and I said: 'Yeah, no problem.'

"What he didn't know was that I went straight to my hotel room and put my ankle in the biggest bucket of ice you've ever seen. But that was the sort of idiocy that went on. In my first ever training session at the club he made me put John O'Hare on my back and run through a field of waist-high stinging nettles. Where else would that happen? I was in my shorts shouting blue murder and wondering what on earth I was doing. Then he had me picking wild mushrooms for him. 'If you find any magic mushrooms, stick them in too,' he called out. The guy was a one-off."

He has equal measures of admiration for Taylor. "I'm a bit disappointed there has been no room made for Peter's name at the City Ground. Anyone who worked with the pair of them knew how important Peter was, so I'm surprised they haven't found somewhere for his name. Clough has a stand named after him, and fair enough, but just a little corner for Peter would be nice.

"He played a bigger part than he was given credit for. He was a natural comedian, brilliant at lifting the mood when people were feeling uptight. They never socialised but, as a managerial duo, it was like chemistry. Peter's role tends to be forgotten but I'm sure Cloughie is up there [he points to the sky] wishing they had made friends and regretting the way they fell out."

Would Clough have any other regrets? "Well, he broke us up too quickly. Liverpool's success was about changing one player each year. But Forest got rid of Frank Clark, Archie Gemmill, Kenny Burns and several others in the space of two seasons after the European Cups. It was too much and the team was never the same again."

His own departure remains a source of irritation. "You knew with Cloughie that when you reached 30 he'd start looking elsewhere, but I was still surprised when he called me into the office and said that he wanted a younger team. 'I'll be honest with you because I know that's how you want it,' he said, 'I don't think at the start of next season you're going to be my centre-half.'

"I said: 'Thanks a bloody lot.' I was 31 but I was convinced I had at least one more season left in me."

# DEEP INTO THE FOREST

Getting Clough to change his mind was a challenge more difficult than nailing a jelly to the wall. "He said he would help me get a player-manager's job so he did an article in the *Sun* saying: 'Larry Lloyd will be one of the all-time great managers, blah, blah, blah'. A few offers came in - Bristol City, Millwall - and off I went to Wigan in the old Fourth Division.

"This was the same week we were in Tokyo to play the World Club Championship game and lost 1-0 against Nacional Montevideo of Uruguay. I came back and played against Rochdale on the Saturday as manager of Wigan. And we lost 1-0 again. So I had two 1-0 defeats that week, one against the top club in the world and one against Rochdale. I wasn't sure what the hell I had done.

"But the thing that disappointed me was that Cloughie replaced me with Willie bloody Young. Okay, he was a steady player. But he was only a year younger than me and a lot slower. Clough had told me he wanted to reduce the age of the squad and then he brought in Willie Young! I mean, what kind of decision is that?"

He went from Wigan to Notts County ("they never accepted me") before leaving football to go into the pub trade, taking over the Stage Door in Nottingham city centre, where in Clough's words he was "the only landlord who was bigger and wider than his own pub."

Lloyd's outspoken views made him perfect for local radio but, despite his popularity, it is also fair to say that his controversial comments were to be his downfall.

"I used to speak my mind and when the fans rang in to have a go at Platt I would never cut it out. They'd be slaughtering Platt, slagging off his signings, and I would be sat there smirking: 'Thanks for your comments, Ryan, next caller . . .'

"I was on holiday in Cyprus and they rang to ask me to go into the office when I got back. I had put their figures up 60 per cent, the biggest increase they ever had, so I presumed they wanted to give me a new deal and a big pay rise.

"Instead, it was this guy from London. I had never met him before and he said straight away: 'David Platt will not have anything to do with this radio station while you're working here.

I'm sorry but we don't require your services any more.' And unknown to me Garry Birtles was waiting round the back to take my slot."

Lloyd has lost touch with many of his old teammates since moving to Spain, where he briefly ran a bar and is now involved in property, and it is sad to report his friendship with Birtles may have suffered irreparable damage.

"I've fallen out with him. Big-style. I'm not upset about him getting the job, but I am that he didn't have the courtesy to ring me when they were offering him it. I've had him about it but I've not seen Platt. Not yet, anyway. But, as I say, what goes around comes around, and I see he hasn't got a management job any longer.

"Stuart Pearce used to tell me how after England games all the lads would go for a drink and Platt would always be the other side of the bar with the FA committee members. All the lads would be looking at him, shaking their heads, while he was buying the directors' drinks. Eeurgh! He's just a horrible man. He's a dickhead, and that's on the record."

# NINE

# Nigel Clough

*I scored 20-odd goals in one season at Forest.*
*I wouldn't have got half of them if it wasn't for Nigel.*

**Teddy Sheringham**

STEVE BRUCE TELLS a story about a football dinner a few years ago. The drink was flowing, the jokes were flying and some of the most important names in the game were swapping stories, swigging wine and slapping backs at the end of another long season.

Bruce was in good spirits as he excused himself to pay a quick visit to the gents. Stood by the urinals, he even found himself humming away as he unzipped his flies. Behind him he heard the door to the lavatories swing open but he didn't really pay much notice. Why should he? But then - whack! - with an almighty blow to his back Bruce found himself propelled into the by-now-half-full urinal. Dazed and confused and, quite frankly, trying not to soak the front of his trousers, he turned round to find a finger being wagged in his direction.

*"Young man, that's for kicking my Nigel as many times as you did. Now carry on . . ."*

\* \* \*

Nigel Clough grew painfully accustomed to opponents leaving the imprints of their studs on his calves, because any clued-up centre-half knew that by taking out Forest's No 9 the entire team could be rendered virtually impotent. Clough was the core of the side that reached Wembley six times from 1989 to 1992, always available to take the ball with his back to goal and spread the play with one of those marvellously perceptive passes.

# NIGEL CLOUGH

To find a Forest player who scored more goals the historians would have to trawl through the record books before picking out the name of Granville Morris at the turn of the 20th century. But it was Clough's capacity for dissecting opposition defences that made him such a feared opponent. It is left feet that are usually called educated - but his right could have had an MA.

He is also, genuinely, one of the most engaging and likeable personalities in a sport that once prompted the great cricket commentator John Arlott to calculate the "bad guys outnumber the good 'uns by about 200 to one." Hence the spontaneous standing ovation when, a day after his father passed away, he brought himself on as a substitute for Burton Albion in a Conference match at Barnet.

There is even a chart-busting hit (well, sort of) dedicated in his honour and given away free in the sadly-now-defunct *Brian* fanzine. 'Give Him a Ball' was a B-side on 'Stupid Kid' (No 1 in the indie charts in April 1993) by The Sultans of Ping FC, a Cork-based band whose lead singer Niall O'Flaherty is a lifelong Red. The Sultans, who had another song called '1979' (inspired by guess which momentous event of that year?), even got away with revealing their allegiance to Clough during gigs in Leicester and Derby.

*"Give him a ball and a yard of grass / He'll give you a move with a perfect pass / Give him a ball and a yard of space / He'll give you a move with godly grace / He's a nice young man with a lovely smile."*

The nice young man is also turning out to be a more than capable manager in his own right. Under his tuition Burton Albion have been transformed into one of the most upwardly mobile clubs outside the professional game, winning back-to-back promotions to the Conference and playing a passing game that was widely thought to be impossible in the blood and thunder, occasionally thud and blunder, world of non-league football.

So it is strange to turn up for our early-evening appointment at Burton's Eton Park and discover that a man who is as popular here as Sir Bobby Robson in Newcastle and Sir Elton John in Watford does not even have his own space in the club car park. Everyone from the commercial director to the main sponsors seems to have an allotted place marked out in capital letters. But when Clough pulls up in his Toyota hatchback he has to make do with finding a space wherever there is one.

It is tempting to wonder what his father might have made of it. "You couldn't imagine Brian Clough getting that sort of treatment," cackles the man in a luminous green jacket by the main door.

Probably not. In fact, definitely not. But the Cloughs were always poles apart temperamentally. One was famed for tackling everything in his life with both guns loaded, a man who specialised in cutting down to size the pompous, the pretentious, the over-high and the far-too-mighty. The other quickly learned the value of discretion, reads the *Independent*, cites apple juice as his favourite drink and, in a managerial sense, has never hurled a teacup in his life.

It is difficult, for example, to imagine the younger Clough aiming a right hook at a few celebratory pitch-invaders in the same way the older one did after Lee Chapman scored four times to help Forest beat QPR 5-2 to reach the League Cup semi-finals in 1989.

Neither could you picture Clough junior spitting on one of his players, as his father once did on Darren Wassall's hand. Or asking pointed questions about the private life of a prospective new signing, as happened to Gary McAllister when he turned at the City Ground in cowboy boots. Or standing in the queue at his local supermarket offering to pay for everyone's shopping - once a regular sight at the Allestree Co-op in Derby.

There is not an occasion on public record when Clough junior has openly courted controversy or been guilty of upsetting anyone with a careless throwaway remark. Quiet and unassuming, Nigel has always taken more after his mother Barbara than the man who doubled up as his father and employer. Sitting in the Albion Suite at Eton Park he is everything you would expect - polite, hospitable and no vaporous clichés. On the next table his son William is decked out in full England kit. "Forest fan?" I ask. "Burton," replies Dad, slightly put out.

# NIGEL CLOUGH

He has apologised in advance in case his memory for detail lets him down but he need not have worried. It soon transpires he has a near-encyclopaedic knowledge of Forest's last 30 years. From his own playing career he can recall in minute detail the matches, the goals, the emotions. And when he thinks even further back he can remember sitting beside his father in dug-outs the length and breadth of the country - a starry-eyed boy getting the best seat in the house and his face on *Match of the Day* every Saturday night.

"It was always straightforward picking which team to support," he explains. "It went, in order, Derby, Brighton, Leeds - very briefly - and then Forest. Once Dad came to Forest they were the club for me."

He was eight when Brian Clough waltzed into the City Ground, a boisterous kid with a blue duffle jacket and missing front teeth. Very soon his bedroom walls were plastered with posters of John Robertson, Ian Bowyer and Martin O'Neill. He can still remember the thrill of his heroes affectionately tousling his hair and calling him by his first name. And at Woodlands Comprehensive in Allestree, a mile or so from the Clough residence in picturesque Quarndon, he was the envy of his classmates as he came back, bleary-eyed but happy, from mysterious-sounding foreign destinations.

"I was growing up in Derby, going to school there and my dad was manager of Forest while they were dominating Europe . . . it led to some interesting moments, that's for certain. I used to get all sorts of stick and there weren't too many other Forest fans around to back me up. The best thing I can say is that it was character-building. But it didn't put me off supporting them, even in the dark days of the old Second Division.

"The club were getting crowds of 7,000 to 10,000 and flirting with relegation when Dad took over. It was pretty desperate but then things just took off.

"There were some unbelievable memories - thing I'll never forget. People go on about the European Cup final in 1979 being disappointing, that it was only Malmo we were playing and that we should have won by a greater margin.

"But I always say: 'Well, what about the teams we'd beaten to get to the final?' Liverpool were rampant in those days yet they couldn't score a goal against us in two games. I'll never forget beating them 2-0 at the City Ground, Garry Birtles running his heart out and Colin Barrett's goal.

"After that, the whole of Europe was taking notice of Forest and we were sweeping past everyone we faced. They weren't one-nils, you know. We beat AEK Athens 5-1 and Grasshoppers Zurich 4-1. And what about the semi-final against Cologne? Look at the players they had. Those matches stand out more than the final. In fact, I can remember Ian Bowyer getting the winner in the away leg as though it were yesterday. That team . . . they never got the credit they deserved."

The younger Clough made his television debut at the age of seven, perched on Brian Moore's knee and smiling cheekily as his father tried to explain an 8-2 home defeat for Brighton against Bristol Rovers 24 hours earlier. At Derby Dave Mackay took him under his wing and worked on the youngster's skills in the old 'shooting box' at the Baseball Ground. And at Forest he was allowed to join in six-a-sides on his school holidays.

"I'd look at the players and wonder what it must be like to be involved for real," he recalls. "What an era that was. Even now there are times when I think to myself that I wish I had been born five years earlier. I'm not saying I would have been good enough to play in the teams that won two European Cups but just to have been around as a player would have been pretty special."

Clough was 18 by the time he signed for Forest, having made a handful of appearances for Heanor Town, as well as turning out for his brother Simon's team, AC Hunters, in Derby's Sunday league.

"Dad would come down every Sunday afternoon to watch us," he remembers. "And I still used to turn out for AC Hunters even after I had started playing for Forest. I was on non-contract terms at Forest so there would be times when I played on a Saturday afternoon at the City Ground and then 24 hours later I would play on a parks pitch in Derby. It was unusual, to say the least, but I really quite enjoyed having two teams - and I took them both as seriously.

"Even when I signed my first professional contract I would go back every Sunday to run the line for AC Hunters. In the end I'd actually become quite a good linesman! But if you can imagine the stick I used to get at school it used to pale into insignificance compared to being a Forest player, the son of Brian Clough, standing in as a linesman in Derby. You had to pretend you were deaf sometimes but it was all light-hearted stuff. Or most of it, anyway."

Practising selective hearing must have been useful preparation for his nine years as a Forest player. Not only did Brian Clough never refer to "the centre-forward" by his first name, even to his backroom staff, he was so intent on showing there would not be any preferential treatment there were times when he went too far with his criticisms.

"Can't you pass a ball? Can't you head a ball? Hey, what's your shirt number?"

"Number nine."

"Well, number-nines are meant to score goals, aren't they?"

At times it was so relentless that senior players such as Garry Birtles and Stuart Pearce plucked up the courage to confront the manager about it. "I went too far," Clough admitted in *Walking on Water*. "I'd be quick to criticise him on the training ground or in the dressing room. In fact, I treated him worse than the other players. I was always looking for that bit more and, worst of all, I was critical of him in front of the other players."

"I wasn't aware of it at the time," says Nigel, with one of his disarming smiles. "When you grow up with it, I suppose you probably get used to it. So it just felt the norm. But, yeah, if there were problems at half-time he might pick me out first and tell me I was crap."

He shrugs his shoulders. "It was fine. I was just another name on the teamsheet and I wasn't spared rollickings just because I was his son. I'd get my fair share and that was okay with me. And I might get it at home too. At least the other players were spared that."

Clough's situation was unique. Not only did he have to prove he was in the team on merit rather than because of his family name, he also had the added burden of worrying that he would be perceived as a dressing-room spy.

Yet his stylish contributions to the team silenced the cynics and he quickly won over his new teammates, grumbling with the best of them and earning their respect because, in his father's words, "they knew he didn't blab."

"Everybody in the dressing room was delighted when he got in the team," explains Neil Webb. "It didn't matter to us whose son he was. We all knew he was a bloody good player."

"Considering the circumstances I think it worked pretty well," Nigel reflects. "Everybody in the media seemed to make more of an issue of the father-son thing than we probably felt ourselves. To us, it was just a working relationship. I wouldn't call him 'Dad' when we were at work and he wouldn't call me 'son'. Then we'd go home and have a different relationship. The crossover was difficult at times but that was just inevitable and we both got used to it.

"As for proving myself to the rest of the players, I knew he wasn't going to pick me unless I was good enough. And the players respected him enough to know it too. When I joined the club there were experienced pros like John Robertson, Garry Birtles and Ian Bowyer in the team. These guys had won European Cups so if somebody walked into that dressing room and couldn't hack it they would suss it out straight away. They didn't care whose son I was as long as I was doing my job on the pitch and, as far as I know, nobody ever had to hold back when they were talking about him in front of me.

"If it was really a problem I could have left on a couple of occasions. Tottenham wanted to sign me apparently and there were rumours of Italy as well. It came down to my Dad asking if I wanted to go and my reply was always the same - that I was very happy at Forest and very happy working for him."

Could he offer his father advice? "Well, he'd listen every now and then, take a bit in and throw the rest away. But that was fine. Why should I have wanted to work for someone else? Over 18 years what he achieved at Forest was absolutely staggering. We would bump into people in the street and grown men would be overcome with emotion to meet him. They'd say: 'I don't care what happens for the rest of my life but I was there in Munich and

Madrid when we won the European Cup.' It was always very emotional for the supporters to meet him because they knew they would never see anything like that again. So you couldn't fail to be proud."

That pride shone through at his father's memorial service at Pride Park. One suspects the old man would have liked the fact that he had sold out his local cathedral, but most of all he would have liked the speech that Nigel gave on behalf of himself, his brother Simon and their sister Elizabeth, all three of them holding hands.

"He had this ability to understand people," Clough junior told the 15,000 people who had gathered in the sort of weather that Thor himself might have invoked. "He also had the ability to drive us mad at times.

"Most of all, he was our Dad. He has left us with a massive gap in our lives and while there are many words we can't seem to find the right ones to say how much we love him and miss him."

How typical of Nigel to have chosen his words so gracefully. "We appreciate that his death came as quite a shock but he was adamant that his illness be kept within his immediate family," he said, the first tears appearing in his eyes as he stood beneath the rain-soaked awning. "Even within the family he kept from us just how ill he really felt, and when he was in hospital he would admit that he hadn't slept well but didn't want to trouble the nurses and doctors for painkillers."

His voice cracking with emotion, he continued: "We hope the pain is gone now and we're sure he's going to have a bit of input upstairs about who exactly is running the show up there. We know that he'll be feeling he can help. We just hope he's sitting there with some good old friends in the sunshine, looking down and saying: 'Look at those daft old buggers sitting there in the wind and rain.'"

The only other time I interviewed Clough junior his father had actually turned up unannounced, demanding to know a) whether I could spell b) had I got O-levels and c) why I didn't get my hair cut.

It was the eve of Burton's televised FA Cup tie against Hartlepool in December 2003 and a photo-shoot had been arranged at a primary school in the town. While the man who won two European Cups held court, boasting to the kids about his scoring record (251 goals in 274 league games) and threatening to "brain" one boy for getting his age wrong, his son watched shyly from the sidelines, wearing the seen-it-all-before smile he must have perfected over the years. This was supposed to be Nigel's day in the limelight but he could hardly get a word in edgeways.

Briefly out of his father's earshot, it was possible to snatch a quick word. "I don't ask for advice but, funnily enough, I get it anyway," he volunteered. "The general rule is to avoid the telephone for 24 hours after every match, let things calm down with him, because you know he'll have something to say about it. He hasn't changed in that respect."

It was not long before Clough senior decided to gatecrash the interview. "He's shaping up as a good manager, but if there's one weakness it's that he's too comfortable. Everyone tells me what a nice lad he is and I'm getting sick of it, to be honest. Sometimes you have to make unpopular decisions if you want to get on in management. It's not easy, for example, telling someone they're not playing in a European Cup final, as I had to. Martin O'Neill didn't look at me for a month. And Archie Gemmill still doesn't."

This was Brian Clough alcohol-free and at his most engaging. His knees gave him so much discomfort, he explained, he no longer drove. But he looked healthy and happy - and his tongue was as sharp as ever.

"It still bugs me that our Nige never got a better chance with England," he grumbled. "Graham Taylor loved him as a fellow but he never had the courage to use him properly. He'd go halfway round the world then spend the entire match with his backside on the bench. Oh well, he got 14 caps and I suppose he can always say that's 12 more than his old man."

The inability of Clough junior to establish himself as a prolific England striker owed much to Taylor's reluctance to shape the team around him, Forest-style. His debut, a scoreless draw against Chile in May 1989, was a classic example: Clough was partnered by John Fashanu and under rigid instructions to stay high up the field rather than playing his normal game of dropping back to knit together midfield and attack. Under those orders, it is little wonder he did not flourish.

Occasionally the press over-emphasised his lack of pace, but the more perceptive sportswriters appreciated him as one of the most gifted playmakers of his generation, quicker of thought than the vast majority of his opponents and rivalled only by Peter Beardsley in terms of his ability to supply the defence-splitting pass. His understanding with Webb was particularly impressive and his one-twos with a rampaging Stuart Pearce were a potent attacking weapon.

He first wore Forest's No 9 shirt against Ipswich on Boxing Day 1984, with brother Simon employed to chaperone him away from the ground and the waiting media. His first goal arrived in his sixth appearance, a 1-1 home draw with Watford, and he went on to become only the sixth player in the club's history to accumulate a century of goals, finishing with 131 in 412 appearances.

Highlights included scoring twice against Luton Town in the 3-1 League Cup final victory in 1989, a four-minute hat-trick against QPR in 1987 and the last-minute winner in a 3-2 victory at Manchester United in 1986 - a comeback from 2-1 down that was so heroic his father ordered 11 copies of the *Match of the Day* video for the victorious team.

Equally memorable is the killer pass that released Nigel Jemson for the decisive moment of the 1990 League Cup final against Oldham. Or, two years earlier, how about the turn and visionary through ball that enabled Brian Rice to run clear and chip Arsenal's John Lukic in a breathtaking FA Cup quarter-final triumph at Highbury?

"We were never going to eclipse the European Cup winning teams but what we achieved was still pretty impressive. Not many teams go to Wembley six times in four seasons and we did it playing good, attractive football. There was a nucleus of myself, Stuart Pearce, Steve Hodge, Des Walker and Neil Webb and we all loved playing together.

"It was just our bad luck that English clubs were banned from playing in Europe at the time. That was very unfair on Forest. We would have loved the chance to take that step up to the next level."

Any matches stand out? "As a supporter, it was the Cologne game. As a player, it was beating Luton in the League Cup final. Not because I scored two of the goals but because it was the club's first trophy since 1980 and the first for what we thought of as 'our team'. Before then, everyone had talked about the potential. That was the moment that all the promise we had shown over the previous few years came to fruition. And it gave us the confidence to keep going back to Wembley over the next three seasons."

He finished as Forest's top-scorer in the league six times and it was fitting somehow that he should register the final goal of the Brian Clough era - the consolation effort in a 2-1 defeat at Ipswich on the final day of the 1992/93 relegation season.

He winces at the memory. "You can talk about the FA Cup final defeat to Tottenham, losing two semi-finals to Liverpool, and Manchester United beating us in the League Cup final, but those disappointments all pale into insignificance compared to the dejection of being relegated. It was just a horrible feeling for everyone concerned knowing that after 42 games we had not been good enough."

His own sense of anguish was exacerbated by witnessing how his father was scarred by the experience. As Brian Clough's 18th season in charge shuddered to its sad and thoroughly unsatisfactory climax, the worry lines began to stand out on his face like contours on a map. His cheeks were pockmarked and red and his expression was one of bewilderment and fear.

"There was a personal edge to it because I could see how it was affecting my dad. By then, everyone knew he would be retiring and it felt as though the whole football world was desperate for it not to finish that way. But football can be cruel sometimes. Forty years in football would take its toll on anyone and in the last 18 months it caught up with him.

"It was a bad time for him. I just hope that after everything that has happened people remember the better times. After 18 seasons of staggering success nobody should dwell too much on one bad season, and I really don't think they do.

"Put it this way, if someone had offered Forest 18 years of almost unbridled success, including league championships and European Cups, but the flipside was that it would end in relegation from the top division, who would have turned it down? Absolutely no one."

It is not - nor will it ever be - Nigel's way to condemn anybody in public, but he felt so strongly about the way Forest's board mishandled his father's retirement it compelled him to leave the club within a month of relegation becoming a fait accompli.

A shabby episode began with one director, Chris Wootton, taking it upon himself to tell the *Sunday People* that the board was in favour of sacking a manager whose increased reliance on alcohol was said to be having a detrimental influence on his work.

The next day - April 26th, 1993 - news crews from all over the world gathered in the Jubilee Club to hear from the chairman Fred Reacher. In the history of great Forest cock-ups what followed must rank as one of the club's least distinguished hours.

It began with the announcement of Wootton's immediate suspension and then Reacher casually blurted out that Clough would be leaving at the end of the season. Cue pandemonium.

It was supposed to be a secret, of course. Clough had made his decision long before Wootton's grubby dalliance with the tabloids. But the blundering Reacher seemed oblivious to the way the announcement would give credence to Wootton's allegations. Or the demoralising effect it would have on Forest's backroom staff and players to turn up for work and find camera crews demanding instant tributes. "You'll have to tell me what's going on first," was usually their first response.

Clough's family stewed in silence. Then Barbara and her three children - Nigel, Simon and Elizabeth - released a carefully prepared statement castigating the board, and deploring the fact that its most important employee had not even been given the opportunity to break the news to his colleagues and players.

*"He has such tremendous respect and affection for them that anything else would be unthinkable. We were therefore surprised and hurt when we heard on the one o'clock news a statement of his impending retirement at the end of the season. We believe the timing could hardly have been worse. The word used most often in*

*the press this week is 'resignation' rather than 'retirement'. After 40 years we feel disappointed that terms like 'hounded out' should accompany his retirement."*

"Relegation wasn't the issue for me," says Nigel, choosing his words carefully. "Nor was it the fact that dropping down a division might affect my international career. I just felt there were one or two things in the boardroom that I wasn't happy with. As long as that was the case it was right time for me to leave, however hard it was."

A playmaker of Clough's prowess seemed a logical choice for a club with Liverpool's passing ethos but his Anfield career stalled after a promising start and he made only 29 league starts in his two-and-a-half years on Merseyside. He then virtually disappeared from the radar when he signed for Manchester City and it says much for his lack of first-team football thereafter that in all the years since he never played against Forest.

So did he regret leaving? "In some ways, but I maintain it was the right decision at the time. If I hadn't gone to Liverpool I would always have been wondering about what might have been. But once I was at Anfield and things weren't working out as I had hoped, there were definitely times when I wished I could go back to Forest. I thought there might be a chance of being part of the deal when Stan Collymore was sold to Liverpool in 1995 but it never happened."

He was disappointed again in early-1997 after Stuart Pearce, stepping in as caretaker manager after Frank Clark's departure, brought him to the club on a three-month loan deal from Manchester City. "I was hoping it would become a permanent move but Dave Bassett came in and thought he could bring in better players." Hmm. The mind goes back to Neil Shipperley and Dougie Freedman.

Pearce had called his old friend within two hours of agreeing to replace Clark. "If I go back into management the very first person I will ring would be Nigel Clough," he says in his autobiography, *Psycho*. "If you put us in different rooms and asked us questions on football, more often than not we would come up with the same answers. I would know that I could leave everything up to Nigel and come back without having been stabbed in the back. He could run a club from top to bottom."

# NIGEL CLOUGH

They make an unlikely duo - the tattooed ex-punk with the reputation as the dressing-room motivator, and the deep-thinker who would sit quietly towards the front of the team coach, calling out the answers to crossword puzzles when his teammates were stuck.

"He's a quiet person," says Pearce. "But he's a very strong character with a strong inner belief, very much like his father. Nigel, however, is a little more flexible than his dad. While Brian had one or two problems in later life, I don't think you will see Nigel go down that road. He has too strong a personality."

And the evidence is there for all to see at Burton Albion. "You couldn't get a better ambassador for the town," the chairman Ben Robinson tells me. "What he has achieved here has been nothing short of a fairytale."

Across the road a new £5million stadium is taking shape. One of the most stylish teams outside the top four divisions is about to get one of the most stylish grounds. And maybe - just maybe - Nigel Clough will be granted his own parking space.

# TEN

# Neil Webb

*Webby was the first of our little group from Forest to be called into the England squad. He was playing so well he couldn't possibly be ignored.*

**Stuart Pearce**

SIX DAYS A WEEK the bedside alarm goes off at 4.15am. "Don't let anyone tell you otherwise," says Neil Webb. "You never get used to getting out of bed that early. It's a killer, especially in winter. It's pitch dark, freezing cold and you can be sure the car will be iced over. But that's the life of a postman."

Surreal. Webb won 26 England caps. At his peak, he earned £5,000 a week and averaged a goal every three games from midfield. And now here he is, sat in a hotel foyer in Reading, the first flecks of grey appearing in his distinctively dark hair, explaining how he ended up delivering letters for a living.

"When I first started people would say: 'You played for England - what are you thinking of?' But I always knew I would have to work again. Yeah, I was earning good money as a footballer but it's nothing like it is today. These days a four-year contract at an average Premiership club can make you financially secure for life if you are sensible. But I missed out on that. There was no way I could afford not to work again after 35. I had no qualifications to do anything else apart from play football so being a postman made sense. It's a job, isn't it?"

There is a sparkle in his eye, but there are also glimpses of hurt and regret.

When Webb left Forest for Manchester United in July 1989 he was the best creative midfielder in England. But after just four games at Old Trafford he shredded his Achilles heel playing for England against Sweden.

134

Ostracised by Alex Ferguson, he returned to Forest and promptly ruptured his other Achilles.

By his own admission he was never the same player again. "It totally changed me - I went from being a box-to-box midfielder who was guaranteed to get ten goals or more every season to being a holding midfielder who sat in front of the defence."

The sparkle went out of his game. He left Forest and went on the soul-destroying journey into the non-league circuit. Football finally washed its hands of him in 1997. He was 33. "Mentally, it took its toll," he says. "I always expected to play until 35 but I had to finish early - not out of choice but because nobody wanted me."

Perhaps the most unfair aspect is that Webb's career fizzled out so ignominiously it is easy sometimes to forget this was a midfielder with a scoring ratio the equal, if not better, to many strikers in English football's top tier. It can feel like a trick of the mind, for instance, that he held his own against Diego Maradona and Michel Platini in the Football League centenary match against a Rest-of-the-World XI. And it can be overlooked that it was only because of an injury to him that the belching, brilliant Paul Gascoigne had the chance to enthral a worldwide audience in Italia '90. "It's a story of exhilarating highs and excruciating lows," he says.

He joined Forest in the same week as Stuart Pearce, but his first meeting with Brian Clough was a fortnight earlier at a London hotel, the night before Forest played Tottenham on the final day of the 1984/85 season. Clough, ever a tale of the unexpected, had scarcely introduced himself to his prospective new signing when he led him to the players' table. "This young man will be taking your place - or your place - or your place," he said, pointing at them one by one.

Webb, crimson with embarrassment, had not even discussed personal terms and was undecided whether to join Forest or go to Aston Villa, who had matched Portsmouth's £250,000 asking price. Doug Ellis, Villa's inimitable chairman, had partially made up Webb's mind (and that of his wife Shelley) in a bizarre exchange when he inquired about her old A-level results and casually observed that she "wouldn't get into university with those grades." But Webb was unsure about Forest too.

"There were a few strange stories going around," he says. "I'd heard the one about him getting rid of Gary Megson because he had been sick in the toilets before one match."

He had still not made up his mind when they next met. Clough began the meeting by summoning one of the YTS apprentices to clean his trainers. Then he gave poor Shelley short shrift when she tried to contribute to the contract talks.

"Hey, I wasn't talking to you, Little Miss Busy," he snapped.

Webb was getting his first taste of Clough's unique behavioural traits. "We were in his office and I asked if I could sleep on it. He told me to walk round the pitch and come back with a yes or no because there was no way he was letting me leave the ground without an answer."

After a lap of the playing surface he returned with the news that Clough wanted. A bottle of champagne was opened and the manager insisted they went for an Italian meal.

Webb was so over-awed he ended up signing a blank contract. "When I got home I couldn't believe I had been so dim. He could have stuck any terms on that contract. But he didn't and, apart from knocking me down £50 a week, I was delighted. The opportunity to work with him was too good to pass up. Okay, he was a bit weird and wacky. But footballers signed for Brian Clough because he turned average players into internationals."

Webb's serene character helped him ride with the verbal punches that Clough threw at all his players at some stage. There were times when he even managed to challenge the manager's authority. At the end of his first season, for example, the team went on one of their frequent jollies to Cala Millor and, along with Pearce, Webb turned up at East Midlands airport wearing Bermuda shorts, flip-flops and mirrored sunglasses, with their hair greased back. Clough's initial reaction was to send them home before accepting, begrudgingly, that it was all a bit of fun.

"I think he'd mellowed an awful lot by the time I got there," says Webb. "Everyone said how aloof and brash he could be but I never found that at all. Sure, he could get pretty upset if we lost but he didn't talk to us like he once did to the likes of Larry Lloyd and Martin O'Neill."

Like anyone who has worked with Clough, however, there were times when he was bewildered, even horrified, by the unorthodox methods put into practice at the City Ground.

"We had a bad first half at Newcastle once and at the interval he turned to Pearcey. 'Stand up' was the command. So Pearcey got to his feet, with no idea what it was all about. Then Cloughie just punched him in the stomach. Bang! Poor Pearcey was doubled up, winded. We just sat there in stunned silence.

"It was my turn next: 'You as well - stand up'. Well, I knew what was coming so I braced myself and, sure enough, he gave me a dig in the stomach, too. I think he probably realised he shouldn't have done it. A few minutes later, when he had calmed down, he went over to Pearcey, hugged him and then thanked him for not punching him back. I was a bit put out - he never said anything to me."

At Reading and Portsmouth Webb had played either on the right wing or in attack, but Clough converted him into a goalscoring central midfielder whose intuitive understanding with Nigel Clough, perceptive range of passing and impressive stamina (in one game the coach of another club counted him making 23 runs of 40 yards or more) made him ideal for a side like Forest.

It was not always a smooth transition. In one of his first matches, the County Cup final, Webb was keen to ingratiate himself with the Forest fans and tried to chip the Notts County goalkeeper. As the ball sailed over the crossbar, Clough marched to the touchline and signalled for him to be substituted. The game was only 15 minutes old.

"Another time Hans Segers got injured 20 minutes into a match at West Ham. I volunteered to go in goal and even though we lost 4-2, I thought I had done reasonably well. In the dressing room he said: 'No wonder we lost, we've got a guy in goal who hasn't even learned how to play in midfield yet.' Then he dropped me from the next match. I was a bit green and asked him what I had done wrong. He said I had been too keen to go in goal. I didn't volunteer for anything ever again. Or try to chip the goalkeeper."

# DEEP INTO THE FOREST

The 1984/85 season had been a relatively disappointing one for Forest, finishing ninth in the old First Division and failing to make any impression in the cup competitions. But the next campaign ushered in a new era with Webb and Pearce making their debuts. It was also the year that Des Walker and Nigel Clough started to establish themselves. Over the next five years Forest began to play some dazzling football and Webb contributed handsomely.

His finest performance was undoubtedly in the 6-2 demolition of Chelsea at Stamford Bridge in September 1986. Webb scored a hat-trick that day (as did Garry Birtles) to reach his seasonal target of ten league goals after only seven games.

International recognition arrived a year later when he came on as a substitute against West Germany in Dusseldorf, so becoming the 1,000th player to win an England cap. But his personal highlight was the League Cup final against Luton Town in 1989 - Forest's first trophy since the European Cup nine years earlier.

Luton, the holders, went ahead in the first half courtesy of a Mick Harford header, a lead they held to the interval. But Forest emerged for the second half with greater verve and vigour. They equalised when Luton's goalkeeper, Les Sealey, brought down Steve Hodge and Clough scored from the penalty spot. Then Webb put Forest ahead (despite offside claims) and Clough added another.

"That was the match I would pick out," says Webb. "We were nervous in the first half but there was no ranting or raving at half time. The Gaffer simply reminded us that we were better than that, and that we had to show it."

After successive third-place finishes in 1988 and 1989 the consensus was that one or two new arrivals could see Forest mount a serious bid for the championship. But Clough's lingering hopes of a second league title effectively unravelled when Webb chose to leave for Old Trafford.

"It was harder than most people think. The supporters couldn't understand it because we had finished above Manchester United that year. But Bryan Robson was at Old Trafford and that was a big factor.

"Most importantly though - and I know a lot of people might not accept this - it came down to the crowds. Even after we had won the League Cup, the Simod Cup and finished third in the league, we were still not getting big crowds. Our last game of the season (a Thursday-night, 2-1 defeat to West Ham) was around the 20,000 mark, whereas Manchester United would get 55,000 regardless of how they were doing."

As Stan Collymore, Roy Keane and countless others can testify, Forest's fans can be callously unforgiving when they believe they have been wronged, and Webb's defection was regarded as a perfidious act of disloyalty. Forest were seemingly on the cusp of great things (Webb had been joined in the England side by Steve Hodge, Stuart Pearce and Des Walker) while back then Alex Ferguson's team were in a state of turmoil, culminating in a banner being unfurled at Old Trafford: "Three years of excuses and we're still crap - tara Fergie."

Webb's transfer cost United £1.5m, earning Forest a £1.25m profit from the amount they had paid Portsmouth, but the monetary aspect failed to appease the Nottingham public.

"Nobody actually threatened me but I would get people coming up to me in the street and saying: 'Why did you go there, you bloody idiot?' Stuart Pearce used to get one of the fanzines, the *Tricky Tree*, and they were bloody terrible to me. They weren't always that kind when I was still a Forest player, but once I went to Man U I was public enemy number one."

Dubbed 'Fat Wallet', he returned to the City Ground in United's colours for the final home game of the season. "I got absolutely hammered," he recalls. "It was understandable, I suppose, because the fans felt I had let them down but I still wasn't quite prepared for how bad it actually was. Sometimes you can blank out the supporters but not when it's constant abuse from the first whistle to the last.

"I didn't think it would affect me. But it did. Every time I got the ball I was nervous because I felt I had to do something good, and because of that I ended up giving it away more often than not. It was one of my worst games for Man U and we lost 4-0."

A young David Beckham used to clean his boots at Old Trafford, and Webb had looked as though he could join the pantheon of United greats when he marked his debut with a wonderfully taken volley against Arsenal.

# DEEP INTO THE FOREST

He went on to win an FA Cup medal in 1990, supplying the killer pass for Lee Martin to score the only goal in a Wembley replay against Crystal Palace. But his relationship with Ferguson disintegrated over the next two years. "He had a few problems with me and I had a few problems with him - like the time he dropped me [for Mike Phelan] on the morning of the European Cup Winners' Cup final."

Webb was beginning to resent Ferguson's famously volcanic temper (he once fined a player for overtaking him on his way out of the training ground) and their relationship broke down irreparably when he was substituted in a match against Wimbledon. Allegedly, he was then told to fabricate an injury to pull out of England's squad to face Czechoslovakia the following week.

The championship race was delicately poised and Ferguson, seeking United's first title success since 1967, would not entertain the idea of one of his players picking up a real injury on international duty.

What Ferguson had not bargained for was the England manager Graham Taylor ringing Webb's home after hearing about the 'injury' from a journalist. "No, he's fine," the player's mother-in-law told him, oblivious to the almighty row that was about to blow up between the Football Association and Manchester United. "Shelley's just rung. He's perfectly okay."

After several days of allegations, counter-allegations and much gnashing of teeth in Fleet Street the upshot was that the FA announced a new decree that withdrawals had to be substantiated with a doctor's certificate.

Ferguson being Ferguson, he never forgave Webb and an £800,000 move was arranged to take him back to Forest, floundering near the bottom of the newly formed Premiership, in November 1992. In his three years at Old Trafford he had managed only 11 goals in 109 appearances.

Football fans being a fickle lot, Webb was quickly welcomed back by the Forest supporters only for his dire misfortune to strike again.

"I went for a scan and they told me my Achilles was only hanging by a thread, and that I needed an operation. It couldn't have come at a worse time. I missed the rest of the season and watched from the stands as they went down. It was terrible."

This was the beginning of the end. Webb worked slavishly to regain his fitness but he was a desperately depressed convalescent. He had to re-invent himself as player and his weight problems began to accelerate. In the 1993/94 season he figured in only 21 of Forest's 46 league games as Frank Clark's side won promotion. Restored to the top division, Clark decided the one-time England star was yesterday's man. The closest Webb got to the first-team again was a substitute's appearance in an FA Cup third-round defeat of Plymouth Argyle.

There is a lingering grievance. "If I'm being really truthful I think the problem for Frank Clark was that when Clough left I had been championing Martin O'Neill to get the job.

"I thought Martin had done a great job at Wycombe and I said as much to the press and even to the chairman. In fact, how Martin was never given the job I still don't understand to this day. Frank came instead and my face didn't fit after that. Were the two things connected? You'll have to ask him. But that's my suspicion.

"I had some great years at Forest but the way it ended really upset me. The last 18 months really took its toll mentally. I was convinced I was the best passer of the ball at the club, especially as Nigel Clough had just left, and it hurt to have someone like Frank Clark telling me I wasn't wanted without offering a proper explanation. For a season and a half I was kicking my heels in the reserves and that's what upset me more than anything."

Clark had decided Webb's injuries had affected his mobility irreparably. Steve Stone was starting to make a favourable impression and in came two new midfielders, David Phillips and Lars Bohinen. Revealingly, in Clark's autobiography, *Kicking With Both Feet*, Webb does not merit a single mention.

Webb had certainly piled on the pounds. On his rare appearances he heard cries of "Mr Blobby" or the familiar chant of "Who ate all the pies?" At times he played along with the crowd, lifting his shirt and rubbing his stomach. But he was hurting inside.

"The fans appreciated his ability to laugh at himself but I don't think he was laughing that hard," Shelley says in her book

*Footballers' Wives*. "He became obsessed with losing weight. He'd eat nothing all day and then I'd wake in the middle of the night to hear him maniacally riding the exercise bike, and that on top of training and afternoon gym visits. He lost weight but at one point I thought he was losing his mind."

Webb leans back in his chair and nods. "My weight was up and down all the time. I used to try to make a joke of it, but the truth is it made me paranoid. When we used to go to restaurants I was always conscious about what I was eating because I thought the people on the next table might be looking.

"I could only get away with a big meal at Antonio's [the Italian restaurant favoured by Forest's players] on Friday lunchtimes. Usually I was the only person there so I could have some pasta and chill out without having to worry about who might be watching.

"But sometimes when I was getting stick from the fans about being overweight I was able to laugh about it because I didn't think I really was. It's only now when I look back at the pictures that I can see why the crowd used to poke fun at me."

His relegation to the 'stiffs' compounded his unhappiness. In his first spell at the club he had scored 57 goals in 186 appearances. It fiercely hurt his pride that on his return he played only 43 games, scoring six times.

"I couldn't understand what I had done wrong," he says. "It all came to a head when the team went to Jersey for four days. Everyone was weighed and I was a stone overweight. That totally freaked me out. We used to go out on Wednesday and Saturday nights but Frank Clark told the press I wouldn't be going anywhere until I had lost some weight."

Webb adopted a more holistic approach to life. "I did everything he asked. I had salads every day and drank nothing but water and juice. I lost a stone in a month, got my fitness back and was feeling really good about myself again. But I still never got a look-in."

Their relationship suffered more damage when O'Neill tried to sign him on loan at Wycombe. "Clark wouldn't let me go. I asked him why and he said I still had a part to play at Forest and that I was the best passer of the ball at the club. But, again, I still never got a game. That was the final straw."

For many footballers the silence that greets the end of their sporting life is the greatest challenge they will ever face. Webb had brief dalliances with Swindon, Exeter, Grimsby and Aldershot, plus a "nightmare" spell in Hong Kong.

"I even went to the newspapers and offered to train with a club for free, just to be given the chance to prove himself. But nobody wanted me and that hurt. People said I was overweight but I still can't understand why no one would give me a go."

His life went into a downward spiral. At his lowest trough he became so reclusive that his wife Shelley feared he was suffering from clinical depression. "He began to exclude everybody," says Shelley. "He became monosyllabic and the children must have wondered why this morose man was living in their daddy's clothes." In the end, she left him.

Webb's curriculum vitae told prospective employers he had worked for Brian Clough, Sir Alex Ferguson and Sir Bobby Robson but "it didn't help a bit."

He fired off applications to just about every managerial or coaching job that was going, but all to no avail. Every now and then he was granted an interview, like the time at Blackpool when he was drummed out for suggesting they used wingbacks. But sometimes he did not even get a reply.

The hurt faded a little when he went to Weymouth but it lasted only 70 days. He went to Reading Town and again it was short-lived. He took a year out and "got bored." On Saturday afternoons he would sleep so he would not feel football had abandoned him.

He started a delivery job for a friend ("it got me out of the house five days a week") and then picked up an application form to join Royal Mail. "My brother-in-law has been at the Post Office since he left school. So I decided to give it a go."

The early starts were brutal. Webb had to check into Reading's main sorting office at 5am. He earned around £300 a week. "To begin with, I'd drive into work but I was getting there like a zombie. So I started cycling to wake myself up. It worked but it meant I had to be out of bed half an hour earlier. So I went back to the car. By 6am, after four cups of coffee, I'd be all right. It's good exercise and you can be home by lunch for a kip in the afternoon. I'm not embarrassed about it."

His new profession was announced to the world, courtesy of the *Sun*, on Boxing Day, 2002. "This reporter had been camped outside my front door for three days. In the end I invited him in to show him I wasn't penniless. I gave him an interview and then waited three weeks. Nothing. I forgot about it. But then it got to Boxing Day and a mate rang up. 'You'd better get the *Sun* - you're on the front page,' he said. 'You're having a laugh,' I said. I never got on the front page of the *Sun* when I was playing.

"Of course, the interview came out totally different to what I actually said. They belittled me. They even slagged off my house - 'a two-up two-down on a bleak estate', that sort of thing.

"But the guy in the newsagents was great. He said: 'Don't worry about it - I'd break stones for my family.' And that sums it up. You work because you have to for your family. What else do people expect me to do?

"I just felt sorry for my neighbours and all the other postmen across the country. The story belittled my neighbourhood, my house, what I was doing. There are thousands of postmen in this country and it made it sound like their jobs were the lowest of the low. Terrific Christmas, that was."

He is now back in Reading, where he began his career and, aged 17 years and 31 days, became the club's youngest-ever scorer. He has worked on local radio, but now his second wife Dawn has given birth to baby Neo he has left the Royal Mail because he needs "normal working hours."

Ideally, that will come in football. "I haven't got my coaching badges yet and I should do, really. I never wanted to be a manager but I think I could be a good reserve-team manager or a number two - maybe even a chief scout. I've got a good football brain so I'm sure I could be involved somewhere.

"It used to be that you got a job and then took your coaching badges. Now it's the other way around so I suppose I will have to get them to stand any chance. I'm probably too laid back about it, to be honest. I'll probably have to find out if there's something out there first but I'm still hopeful."

He has, after all, been educated by the manager he rates as the best there has ever been.

"Cloughie was a genius but his methods were very simple. The teamsheet went up on Friday lunchtime and we might not see him again until five minutes before kick-off. Players who had never worked for Clough would be amazed at the way he prepared us. Sometimes he'd tell everyone to 'bugger off home' from training just because he didn't think people were trying. Other times he would close down the physio's room for a week because he was fed up of seeing people in there. I had a hamstring strain once, but his attitude was that I wasn't doing him any good so I might as well not bother turning up.

"But he was great at making sure we did not complicate the game. When I went to Manchester United Alex Ferguson was so intense. It was a culture shock, to be honest. At Forest I was used to getting to the ground on match-days at 1.45pm. At Old Trafford I had to be there at 11.45am. We'd have a team meeting for an hour and there was a dossier on our opponents for every game. That was unheard of at Forest."

He is laughing now. "It was mad sometimes. If you go down to the training ground there's a line of poplars. I'm not sure how big they are but they were only six feet tall when we put them in. Mine is somewhere on the left.

"The place was so damn windy Cloughie went to the local garden centre to get them while we were training. Then we had to plant them in a line. 'This will keep the wind out,' he told us. Like I say, it was mad at Forest sometimes."

# ELEVEN

# Ian Storey-Moore

*And the crowd have gone bonkers.*

**Kenneth Wolstenholme**

NOBODY COULD EVER visit the City Ground for an official appointment and accuse Forest of lacking sentimentalism. Inside the main reception the walls are lined with pennants and photographs. Jack Burkitt is being carried shoulder-high with the FA Cup in his hands. Peter Shilton is kissing the European Cup, holding it so preciously it could be made of bone china. Kenny Burns is thrusting the league trophy to the skies. There is even a picture of Chris Bart-Williams scoring the goal that saw Forest return to the Premiership in 1998, albeit for a painfully brief spell. Heady times. Memories of a different century.

Through the double doors, past the bronze bust of Brian Clough, the entire left wall is covered by the picture of Trevor Francis heading in John Robertson's cross against Malmo, the goal that won the European Cup. Francis is about to land on the shot-putters' circle at Munich's Olympic stadium. Not that he cares - he didn't feel a thing.

On the right is the roll of honour for all the Forest players who have won international caps. Almost 100 different names are embossed in gold, from Arthur Goodyer in 1879 to Andy Reid 125 years later. Stuart Pearce's name stands out immediately, with a club-record 76 England caps. Martin O'Neill. Tony Woodcock. Peter Shilton. And then there are the anomalies, players such as Thorvaldur Orlyggson (Iceland: 16 caps) who was a better Scrabble score than he was a midfielder. Or Alan Davidson, who made as many appearances for Australia (five) as he did for Forest.

# IAN STOREY-MOORE

Ian Storey-Moore's office is next door and he would be entitled sometimes to stop in front of that list and wonder what might have been had it not been for Alf Ramsey's reluctance to play wingers. It says much for his outrageous gifts that he eventually forced Ramsey to reconsider, but it is still remarkable that his international career consisted of nothing more than a solitary appearance against Holland at Wembley in January 1970.

The cream does not always rise to the top. Storey-Moore was Forest's George Best - a handsome, brilliantly effective winger who could quicken the step of a supporter en route to a stadium and change the course of any match with a single moment of brilliance. Not that he got anything like the exposure of Best, of course. But in 1966/67 Forest had a side that all but matched Matt Busby's Manchester United and Storey-Moore was the star of the show.

They say nobody remembers nearly men, but that Forest team should never be forgotten. They won 16 and drew four of their 21 home games (losing only to Stoke) only to be pipped to the championship by the great United side of George Best, Bobby Charlton and Denis Law that would win the following season's European Cup. In the title decider Forest lost 1-0 at Old Trafford. A 4-1 trouncing of United at the City Ground, with Chris Crowe scoring a hat-trick, has been lost in the small print now, although it was never much of a consolation to Storey-Moore anyway, particularly after an FA Cup semi-final defeat against Tottenham in the same season.

"It was so nearly the Double," he sighs from behind his desk. "It was just bitterly disappointing to get so far and get nothing. All it would have taken was a couple a different results here and there and maybe a moment or two of better luck and everything could have been so different. Not winning anything with Forest was the biggest disappointment of my career."

His are bitter-sweet memories but the consolation is that he can align himself to one of the most thrilling periods of football in Nottingham in the years BC (Before Clough) - a time when the top-scorer's award kept returning to him like a homing pigeon, and the excitement and the crowds just seemed to grow and grow.

# DEEP INTO THE FOREST

Ultimately, that side may have finished empty-handed but supporters of a certain generation are still entitled to get misty-eyed as they nostalgically think back to the style and panache of Johnny Carey's team, the Trent End choir serenading "Zigger Zagger" Joe Baker and the sight of nearly 50,000 fans crammed into the City Ground.

In the schmaltzy afterglow of England's World Cup success, this was a season that lured the largest crowds Forest have ever had and the sense of provincial pride hung thick in the air even when it became apparent there were be no requirement for extra reserves of silver polish, after all.

"There was just a great feel-good factor throughout the city," says Storey-Moore. "They had not had success here for many, many years and Nottingham was buzzing. In those days they would let kids in over the walls and I remember the place used to be full to the rafters. Forty-nine thousand. Incredible. Bulging at the seams. It was wonderful to be part of, really wonderful, and it was a great team - nobody can take that away from us.

"For one season everything just gelled. We were playing 4-4-2, which was a new system back then, and we had some excellent individual players. Joe Baker, for example was a wonderful footballer. He was priceless, really - extremely quick, always a danger, the sort of player who would put a spark into a drab nil-nil and get a goal out of nothing.

"Terry Hennessey was one of the most cultured centre-halves around, Bob McKinlay was a great player for many years and up front Frank Wignall was a particularly strong forward, so Joe worked off him well.

"Then there was John Barnwell who was the midfield playmaker and Henry Newton, who was another great midfielder, a box-to-box player, extremely strong and aggressive - he would have been ideal for today's game. I would start on the left but I was more or less given a free role, which probably explains why I scored so many goals."

Storey-Moore was the leading scorer in five out of six seasons (even in 1971/72 when he had left the club by February) but

# IAN STOREY-MOORE

1966/67 was his best in terms of goals. A lethal finisher, he managed 25 including a hat-trick against Everton in an FA Cup quarter-final that earned him his own little piece of immortality - a day, he says, that he "will never be allowed to forget, nor want to."

Thirty years on, supporters voted it as their favourite Forest match of all time, trumping two European Cup finals and much more besides. April 8th, 1967, was the pinnacle of a so-near-to-history season, a day when the holders were dispatched from the FA Cup and Storey-Moore's contribution to a mesmerising 3-2 victory secured his place in the pantheon of Forest greats.

It is also the only Forest match to be chosen as one of the 60 most memorable games ever to be played in the British Isles, in a book of that name. Under the title "Some Game, Some Goal, Some Finish" the authors recount how Storey-Moore first equalised, made it 2-1 and then, when a late Jimmy Husband goal had looked like forcing a replay, the lung-splitting climax as Wignall headed the ball down in the box and time seemed to stand still.

Storey-Moore's first shot came back off a defender, the rebound struck the goalkeeper, his third attempt was headed on to the crossbar and at the fourth go, with 49,000 raucous fans looking through the lattice of their fingers, he finally completed his own game of penalty-box pinball by lashing in the winner. Ask anyone who was there, and they will tell you that for one glorious moment it seemed as though the City Ground and Heaven were one and the same place.

"It still has a dreamy quality about it," Storey-Moore recalls of his first-ever hat-trick. "It can be a little embarrassing at times because so many people ask me about it, especially the older supporters, and I've always maintained that our best player that day was Frank Wignall [a half-time substitute for the injured Baker]. Although I scored the goals, he had a wonderful game. He was an ex-Everton player so he probably had a point to prove. I remember he caused them all sorts of problems.

"As for me, everything just fell perfectly that day. The place was packed and the crowd were almost on the pitch by the end.

"The winner arrived so late they had no time to recover, and it was on television in black and white that night, which was quite a rarity. It was just a great game with a great climax. And it says everything that the supporters voted it as the greatest match in the club's history, especially when you consider some of the famous European matches that were overlooked."

More than 100,000 fans queued for tickets for Hillsborough, but FA Cup semi-finals have never been Forest's forte. In fact, it is fair to say Jonathan Ross is better at pronouncing his Rs than Forest are at winning FA Cup semi-finals. From 1879 to 1991 the club were involved in 11 but won only three. And Jimmy Greaves, who managed more goals (29) against Forest than any other club, saw to it that Storey-Moore's journey home from Sheffield to Nottingham would be one of despondency.

"It's every player's dream to get to an FA Cup final, especially in those days when it seemed to matter more than it does now. So that semi-final at Hillsborough was a very bleak day.

"The hard part was that we were really on top for the first 25 minutes. I don't think Spurs had had a kick, and Jimmy Greaves in particular. But with his first real touch he'd put it in the back of the net and I suppose that was Jimmy in a nutshell. After that we never got going and it finished 1-0. I can remember looking at the Kop after the final whistle, staring at the bank of red that was the Forest fans, and just feeling terrible for them."

This was a time when Forest should have sought to close the gap on Manchester United rather than allow it to become a chasm. But the way the team was suddenly broken up has similarities to Clough's dismantling of the European Cup-winning sides, and it pains Storey-Moore to remember how quickly they lapsed back into mediocrity.

"It seems to be an unfortunate trait of Forest's. Over the years it just keeps happening, doesn't it? I can't understand it now and I couldn't understand it then. I've always felt that once you start to sell your better players it's the start of the slippery slope.

"We were unfortunate in one respect because Joe Baker suffered a horrific injury in that Everton game. Joe never really recovered and he certainly wasn't the same player when he came back. So we lost him and then for some obscure reason the powers-that-be started to break the team apart, starting with Henry Newton and Terry Hennessey.

"It was hard seeing your mates leave and I found it inexplicable really. Instead of taking the next step forward and bringing in more players to improve the team we went the other way. That was really disappointing because great things could have happened here."

Instead, with most of their best players sold and Storey-Moore missing 13 weeks of the 1968/69 campaign through another spell of injury, the break-up of the team would have seen them relegated had he not regained fitness to score a brilliant individual goal at Coventry that sent them down with Leicester and QPR.

"The truth is that I shouldn't have played," he says. "It was a terrible ankle injury but they pleaded with me to give it a go and it paid off because going down would have been a disaster."

His abiding memory of that season, however, is the day the Main Stand caught fire against Leeds - and a close encounter with what could have been a real disaster.

"I walked into the tunnel at half-time and was suddenly enveloped in smoke. It was pretty scary. I didn't properly realise what was going on but we were quickly ordered back on to the pitch and when I looked up I could see all the black plumes of smoke.

"I think it was an electrical fault. The stand was mostly made of wood and it was amazing nobody was hurt. The crowd were evacuated, there were fire engines all over the car park and everything in the stand was gone. I lost all my clothes, although they probably weren't worth that much - about two bob, I'd reckon."

Forest moved to Meadow Lane for their next six home games and Storey-Moore scored in every one. In fact, he managed no fewer than 13 goals in the 13 matches (home and away) Forest played while homeless.

"Personally, it went really well. It was one of the most prolific spells in my career. But we didn't win a match and it was a pretty miserable time for the club. By the end we were glad to get back."

Much of Storey-Moore's popularity was not only due to his outstanding talents but because supporters respected his loyalty to Forest at a time when other star players were being enticed away.

Yet his devotion was not due to local origins. Storey-Moore arrived in Nottingham as a skinny 16-year-old who had been brought up in Ipswich before moving with his family to Scunthorpe, where he had trials with Blackpool and Grimsby only to be told on both occasions that he was too flimsy for the muck-and-nettles combat of professional football.

"They were probably right," he says. "I was really small for my age. I didn't start to fill out until I was at Forest and Jack Burkitt, who was working as the reserve team trainer, put me through a rigorous fitness and weights programme."

Beefed up, he signed professional forms in 1962, made his debut in a 2-1 defeat of Ipswich a year later and went on to become the first footballer with a double-barrelled surname to play for England. His performance against Holland was acclaimed in the press and with better luck he might even have marked his debut with a hat-trick, striking the woodwork twice, seeing a shot cleared off the line and finding the net with a header that was ruled out for an earlier infringement.

Sadly, his injuries did not seem to come in threes but 33s. Chosen in the provisional squad for the 1970 World Cup in Mexico, Storey-Moore had reason to be optimistic that his talents were finally being rewarded, only for the fates to decree otherwise.

"The next Forest game was away at Manchester City and I was the victim of a bad tackle, got a really bad injury and was out of the squad - as simple as that," says Storey-Moore, grimacing at the memory. "It was devastating, really. I hope I don't sound bigheaded but I do think I could have won more caps. When I look back I was desperately unlucky with injuries. I remember playing my first game for England, thinking that I'd done reasonably well, and Alf Ramsey saying I would be in the team for the next match. But it all fell apart with that injury."

The perpetrator that fateful day at Maine Road was Arthur Mann with a challenge that, according to one report, "felled his opponent like a tree." Storey-Moore was a lone front-runner at that stage and in the dark ages of over-the-ball specialisation every team had its statutory hatchet-man who, straight from kick-off, invariably targeted him in the knowledge that putting him out of the game would render Forest's forward line virtually impotent.

"It's probably why I had so many injuries. It didn't matter how much skill you had in those days, you had to be tough, as well. If you were a wimp, you didn't get very far, especially if you wanted to score a goal.

"There were some mean players about, people like Ron Harris, Tommy Smith and Norman Hunter. The first chance they'd get to take you out, they wouldn't think twice - bang!

"In that respect, football is totally unrecognisable now. The referees were so much more lenient you had to strangle or shoot someone before they would even consider booking you for their first foul. Nowadays the strikers get far more protection but I wasn't that fortunate."

Since Frank Clark's final days at the club Storey-Moore has been operating as Forest's chief scout, but the paradox is that there was a time when Brian Clough was manager that he was about as welcome at the City Ground as Robert Maxwell.

The reasons for this very one-sided antipathy stemmed from Clough's failed, and rather farcical, attempts to pinch Storey-Moore from under Manchester United's nose when he was Derby manager in 1972.

Somehow, somewhere, Clough's antennae had picked up on the fact that Forest were willing to sell their most prized asset and that Storey-Moore had met Frank O'Farrell, the then United manager, at Edwalton Hotel without agreeing terms.

Within the hour Clough had matched United's £200,000 offer and arrived at Edwalton (driving past O'Farrell on the way) to promise Storey-Moore the money he wanted. He then whisked him away to Derby to sign the registration forms.

Storey-Moore found himself "slightly in awe" of Clough. Derby were playing Wolverhampton Wanderers at the Baseball Ground the next day and just before kick-off the "new star signing" was brought out on the pitch and introduced to the crowd.

"As soon as I signed the forms I thought I was a Derby player. Mr Clough, for one, insisted I was - and when he insists you are, you usually believe him. But Forest had suddenly got the jitters and wouldn't sign the release papers because they didn't want another player going to their fiercest rivals. There had been a few others who had already gone in the same direction and they were frightened that if they let me go as well the fans might erupt.

"This was unknown to me at the time, of course. So I was paraded round the Baseball Ground, waving to the fans, thinking it was a done deal and blissfully unaware of what was really happening. It wasn't until the Monday that it came to light that Forest would never let it go through. I switched on the radio and instead of the usual news about wars or strikes the main story was all about me.

"I was still with Clough at the Midland Hotel in Derby and things were getting increasingly tetchy. When he found out for certain he ended up literally throwing the forms at me and he never spoke to me for a long, long time after that. In fact, I think there might have been an unofficial ban on me coming to Forest when he started here as manager.

"He never forgave me but the truth is that I was happy to sign for Derby. Clough was such a great manager it would have been a privilege to play for him. And I actually missed out on a championship medal because they won the league that year."

To understand why Clough's reaction was so extreme it is important to note a) the talent of the player who had slipped through his fingers and b) when it came to transfer dealings he had no peers, and was wholly unaccustomed to missing out on anyone. This was the man who kipped down on the settee at Archie Gemmill's house after the Scottish midfielder had asked to sleep on a move from Preston to Clough's Derby.

So Clough, that famed grudge-bearer, took it as a personal affront when he learned that Matt Busby, then a director at Old Trafford, had travelled to Storey-Moore's house in Bingham to persuade him to sign for United, after all.

An apoplectic Clough blamed Forest and fired off a four-page letter of complaint to Alan Hardaker and the Football League committee. His mood was not helped when Sam Longson, the Derby chairman with whom he would spectacularly fall out, immediately dissociated himself from

# IAN STOREY-MOORE

Clough's complaints, apparently fearful of upsetting such an influential figure as Hardaker. Forest were subsequently absolved of any blame and Derby were fined £5,000 for parading a player who had never belonged to them.

In his autobiography Clough wrote: "Even I hadn't bargained for the kind of shit that hit the fan. You couldn't mess with Manchester United, the great Matt Busby's club, in those days. We were left waving goodbye to Storey-Moore as he departed for Old Trafford and our tails were very definitely between our legs."

"The whole episode was just embarrassing," says Storey-Moore. "I was caught up in the middle of it all and took most of the flak but the truth was that I had done nothing wrong.

"Nothing like that would ever happen these days. Everyone's got an agent now, whereas back then I was left alone to handle a move involving a record transfer fee. It was the first time I had been involved in anything like that and I didn't really enjoy the experience."

Seeing him leave for Old Trafford rather than the Baseball Ground only partially diluted the sense of disappointment for Forest's supporters. He had scored 118 goals in 272 appearances and, deprived of their hero, the fans protested with their feet.

A paltry crowd of 9,872 watched the first home match since his departure, less than half the attendance for the previous game. The mood was not helped when, in a moment of Alan Partridge tragicomedy, the half-time public announcer cheerfully revealed that Storey-Moore had just scored for United on his debut. Forest lost 2-0 to Ipswich and at the end of the season they were relegated. Once again the City Ground felt like a cathedral with nothing to worship.

Storey-Moore scored in each of his first three games for United but in 1974 he was forced out of league football by an ankle injury he aggravated in the club's gymnasium. The legacy is that he now suffers from arthritis - something he partly puts down to that Coventry match in 1969 and "all the injections they gave me."

He has subsequently opened a newsagent's, a bookmaker's chain and used to run the Wheatsheaf pub in Bingham, where the regulars included Roy Keane and Steve Stone.

# DEEP INTO THE FOREST

"Footballers back then never left the game with a lot of money," he says wistfully. "Nowadays if a player has a good career he can retire immediately, but we were paid a relative pittance - at Forest I got £40 a week with a £4 win bonus - so we had to get out into the big, wide world and fend for ourselves.

"I got involved in non-league football at Burton Albion and Shepshed Charterhouse but, again, the salary was derisory - about £50 a week - so I had to look at some other business interests."

Being the club's chief scout must be a tricky business given the cash-flow problems - i.e. poverty - that have existed at the City Ground since the financial meltdown outside of English football's top tier. "Because the club have had limited funds it's not so much about finding new players to sign," he explains. "It's more about watching the opposition, analysing their tactics and putting together a match report for the manager.

"It can take up to four hours just to write a single report. You have to look at the shape of their team, their set-pieces and where their strengths and weaknesses lie. The manager will then decide how we mark at corners etc., write out everyone's responsibilities and stick them up on the dressing-room wall. We try to do it as professionally as possible."

A small thing, maybe, but it is a pity there are no pictures of Storey-Moore on the City Ground walls. The hat-trick goal against Everton, perhaps. Or the time in 1971 when he took the ball from 25 yards inside his own half and ran the length of the pitch before depositing it past Arsenal's goalkeeper Bob Wilson. In terms of an individual effort, there has possibly been only one occasion to compare since: Tommy Gaynor slaloming through the entire Huddersfield team in a League Cup tie at Leeds Road in 1989.

These are moments those who were privileged enough to see first-hand will never forget. Storey-Moore's international career might have been painfully short but few players have ever illuminated the City Ground with such style.

# TWELVE

# Archie Gemmill

*As a player he was superb. As a man, I'm not sure
who disliked him the most - those who worked with him
or those who played against him.*

**Brian Clough**

THE MIDLAND HOTEL in Derby has clearly seen better days. In its heyday Brian Clough used to bring Derby County's prospective new signings here to show them the city's equivalent of the Ritz. Yet, three decades on, the glitterati have moved on. There are still flashes of 1970s grandeur, but there are also lipstick stains around the top of my glass and a thin layer of dust on the grand piano. Across the road is a 'massage parlour' (yeah, right!) called Bubbles, and the type of late-night eateries that Mike Skinner, aka The Streets, refers to as "shit-in-the-tray merchants."

It would be easy to take a cheap shot about the apparent decline in standards mirroring that of Derby's football team. But it is difficult to gloat too much when, on the winter's day Archie Gemmill arranges a rendezvous in the hotel bar, Forest are languishing in the bottom three of the Football League Championship, in danger of being dragged into the third tier of English football for the first time since 1951.

The prospect of a regular local derby against Chesterfield serves only to whet the appetite for an afternoon of nostalgic reminiscences about the days when Forest could rightly claim to be the greatest team in Europe, and a balding, stocky little fellow from Paisley established himself as one of the most formidable midfielders of his generation.

One problem: when Gemmill arrives he is such a "wee man" he cannot see over the back of my chair. He promptly leaves the

157

bar, assuming I am late, and waits outside in the hotel foyer. And after ten minutes he decides enough's enough . . . and drives home.

When I ring him an hour later his explanation does not make me feel any better.

"I thought I saw somebody behind the piano," he explains. "You were only a few feet away - but I thought it was a girl."

*A girl?*

This is not how I imagined the interview would turn out. In fact, it is a mess. Yet Gemmill volunteers to drive back and, as he sips on a cappuccino and turns his thoughts back to life at the City Ground, he is so candid and generous with his time I begin to feel slightly ashamed that, for no particular reason whatsoever, I had worried he would be the most difficult interview of the lot. No question is off bounds and the tough-guy exterior melts as he reflects upon Clough's death. "I feel like I have lost a true friend, a wonderful man," he says.

Gemmill's affection for his former manager might surprise readers of Clough's two autobiographies, in which he fluctuated wildly from describing the Scot as "absolutely brilliant" to depicting him as the sort of "miserable little bugger" who should hang a neon sign around his neck warning: Do Not Disturb.

There were times when Clough seemed to take immense pleasure needling the man he called 'The Nark', describing him as "grim-faced and intense" and coming to the conclusion that Gemmill's inability to establish himself as a successful manager owed to "personality rather than ability."

Yet here's the funny thing: Old Big 'Ead developed a closer relationship with The Nark in his later years than with any of his other players.

It might not always have been apparent and, of all the relationships between Clough and his players, theirs was always one of the most difficult to analyse. Yet Gemmill was a strong enough character to cope with the indiscriminate lash of Clough's tongue, and the sadness in his eyes tells its own story. "I'm just glad the memorial service gave him such a great send-off," he says. "The service was wonderful and the speakers captured the mood perfectly. Nigel, in particular, did a brilliant job."

# ARCHIE GEMMILL

It was an odd alliance. Gemmill makes no bones about the fact that there were long spells in his playing career when he took exception to Clough's bizarre behavioural traits. He resented the times before crucial matches when Clough refused to let him go to bed because he wanted an audience for his late-night anecdotes. He grew wearily accustomed to Clough poking fun at his occasional dourness. And he has harboured a long, smouldering grudge since being left out of the 1979 European Cup final.

Yet Gemmill visited Clough on a near-weekly basis when his mentor/tormentor (sometimes it was difficult to differentiate) settled into retirement amid the rolling hills of Derbyshire's amber valley.

There were times when Clough's knees would not allow him to drive, and Gemmill would act as his unofficial chauffeur. On other occasions they would sit in Clough's garden, talking football, exchanging gossip, arguing over who had the best lawn. Their relationship might have been tempestuous at times but a sense of mutual respect brought them closer than either probably ever imagined.

"I've seen a softer, more generous side to Brian Clough," says Gemmill. "Everybody thinks of him as this brash and opinionated football manager who could sometimes say too much. Well, he could be like that. But they didn't know the man like I did. I knew the other side of him too - how he would cook dinner for the old people near where he lived, how he helped out in hospices, how he visited kids in hospitals. He was idolised as a manager, but if people knew the other side of him he would have been loved even more."

Gemmill came to Forest in the embryonic stages of the championship-winning 1977/78 season in the same spending spree that saw Peter Shilton sign for a record £270,000 from Stoke City and Kenny Burns for £150,000 from Birmingham City. Peter Taylor had heard through the grapevine that Gemmill had fallen out with Derby's manager Tommy Docherty and, using this information to their advantage, Forest offered £20,000 in a cash-plus-player exchange involving the England under-21 goalkeeper Jim Middleton, who had lost his place to Shilton. Gemmill would go on to figure prominently in almost all of Forest's success over the next two years.

# DEEP INTO THE FOREST

Middleton, in stark contrast, spent the same period fighting to keep his place while Derby struggled to save themselves from relegation. "The thing is, and I have to stress this, I went to Forest expecting success," says Gemmill. "They might have just come out of the old Second Division but I had worked with Brian Clough and Peter Taylor before. So when they told me I was the final piece of the jigsaw in building a championship-winning team I believed them.

"It would be unthinkable now to imagine a team winning the league the season after they had been promoted, but it didn't surprise me one iota that we were so successful. As far as I was concerned, it was a matter of when, not if, we would win the league. There were never any ifs.

"They were an exceptional bunch of lads. There was a great team spirit and it was impossible not to have absolute faith in every player in the team. There might have been people at the club who you wouldn't particularly get on with, but if you were playing on a Tuesday night away from home and it was peeing down with rain you knew there were ten other players who would stand up for you, no matter what.

"That all came down from the boss. He was a powerful man who knew exactly what he wanted and he nearly always got it. I have no hesitation whatsoever in saying this: Brian Clough was a genius."

I remind him of a quote he was reputed to have made about Clough during their days together at Derby:

"*I hate the bastard sometimes, but I would give him my last half-crown.*"

"I'm not sure they're the exact words I used but that would be a pretty fair assessment from my playing days. There were times when you would feel particularly hard done by and full of resentment. But you would always find yourself sticking up for him and you would give every ounce for him on the football field.

"It's very difficult to sum up in just a few sentences, but the man was an enigma. He was a law unto himself and he sailed very close to the wind a few times, but he was so good at his job everything just fell into place."

# ARCHIE GEMMILL

Gemmill was a fast, scurrying midfielder, tenacious in the challenge and with energy to burn. No player was more inspirational, particularly when the going got tough. "Archie could be nasty when he wanted," Tony Woodcock once said, "you need people like that in a successful team."

Clough certainly liked his midfield players to have a snap in their tackle and Gemmill's passion and skill epitomised the Forest side of that era, even if his career in Nottingham was to get off to a false start. Clough had paid Gemmill the ultimate compliment by favouring him ahead of John McGovern for his debut, a 1-1 home draw against Norwich City, but the manager was unsparing in his post-match criticisms and promptly dropped him, saying he had picked up "too many bad habits" during his final days at Derby.

"The real Archie Gemmill must have been put in chains in recent years," Clough told the newspapers. "He's forgotten all his good habits, playing the ball back to defenders all the time. He wouldn't have been allowed to play like that when I was at Derby and he won't play that way here. We've got a lot of work to do with him."

"That was to let everyone in the dressing room know who was the boss," smiles Gemmill. "I was the new signing who had come in and taken the captain's place in my first game. So he probably wanted to bring me down a peg or two in front of everyone. Everybody was thinking: 'Jesus, if the captain's been dropped my job's not safe.' The boss was simply making sure there was no complacency."

Gemmill's retort was softly stated but brilliant and sustained and, alongside McGovern, he swiftly became the fulcrum of the side.

To pinpoint his best individual display it is probably necessary to go back to the famous 4-0 victory at Manchester United in December 1977, when his selfless running and visionary passing created a succession of chances for Tony Woodcock and John Robertson. *The Match of the Day* cameras were at Old Trafford that afternoon, as they were for Arsenal's visit to the City Ground the following month when he started and finished a move spanning the entire length of the pitch for a magnificent breakaway goal. It was the pièce de résistance in a 2-0 victory and earned the indefatigable Scot the goal-of-the-season award, one of only two occasions when a Forest player has won the title - the other being Johnny Metgod for his cannonball free-kick against West Ham in April 1986.

Forest were en route to winning the league by seven points (in the days of two points for a win) although Gemmill was cup-tied, along with Shilton and David Needham, for the League Cup triumph against Liverpool that season, having played in an earlier round for Derby.

In an era when the League Cup was considered only marginally less important than the FA Cup it was a source of constant irritation to Gemmill, but he made up for it in the league where his performances were the equal of any player in the country.

"Gemmill comes high on the list of our best signings," Clough said in later years. "How we managed to get a player of such courage and talent for so small a price I will never know. We got him for buttons and he was the best pro we had on our books. Better than Shilton. Better than Burns. His approach, his attitude and his all-round know-how were precious. He never gave less than his maximum and his pace, movement and tackling ability were astonishing. In fact, if he had cost £1m, he would have been worth it."

Gemmill was soon captaining the Scotland side (he won 43 caps in total) and the man with size-six feet will always be fêted in his home country for conjuring up the most illuminating moment of the 1978 World Cup in Argentina.

Even the average American - well, those who have seen *Trainspotting* anyway - must be aware of the mesmerising way the diminutive playmaker picked up a loose ball on the right of the Dutch penalty area, came inside Wim Jansen's lunge, beat Ruud Krol on the outside, pushed the ball between Jan Poortvliet's legs and lifted it over the advancing goalkeeper Jan Jongbloed.

Holland's classy defenders were made to look as mobile as a row of stalagmites and Gemmill's jinking, brilliant effort in a 3-2 victory at the San Martin stadium in Mendoza has not only been voted the best Scottish goal of all time but came seventh in a FIFA poll to find the best goal in World Cup history.

# ARCHIE GEMMILL

It was not enough, of course, for Scotland to qualify from the group stages but the importance of that moment north of the border can be accurately gauged by the fact that 23 years later the Scottish Dance Youth Company choreographed a ballet entitled *The Nutmeg Suite* in honour of "15 seconds of Total Football."

In an interview with the *Guardian* the director Andy Howitt revealed how his grandfather had died of a heart attack three minutes after Gemmill's moment of immortality. "He had already had two heart attacks, this goal went in and he cheered and told me: 'We will win the World Cup.' The shock was so great for him."

The most famous tribute, however, comes courtesy of that scene in *Trainspotting*. Renton has been indulging in some passionate love-making and when he finally comes up for air he gasps: "Christ, I haven't felt that good since Archie Gemmill scored against Holland in 1978!"

"I saw that at the pictures and I had absolutely no idea what was coming," laughs Gemmill. "John McGovern and myself were in charge at Rotherham at the time and after a match one weekend we took all the players to the cinema. As I say, I had no idea what was in store but you can imagine how it went down . . . the place was in uproar."

His irresistible form extended from the World Cup (the less said about Scotland's failure to beat Iran the better) to the 1978/79 season, most notably in the European Cup showdown against Liverpool at Anfield when, leading 2-0 from the first leg, his ubiquitous performance helped keep the return leg scoreless and led to Clough identifying him for special acclaim afterwards.

Accolades from the great man were not to be treated lightly but Forest's run to the final against Malmo would end in bitterness and resentment for the inspirational Scot, and the gravest disappointment in his distinguished career.

Gemmill had ruptured his groin in the first leg of the semi-final against Cologne at the City Ground. For six weeks he worked feverishly to regain his fitness, and then a week before the big day he was pencilled in for the County Cup final against Mansfield.

# DEEP INTO THE FOREST

"I was supposed to play the full match and I should have realised something was wrong when I turned up at the ground and saw I was only on the bench," recalls Gemmill. "The boss wasn't at the game, so I had a word with Peter Taylor and he assured me he would be happy as long as I could come through 20 minutes. I probably played nearer half an hour, and I came through it all fine so I travelled to Munich convinced I would be in the team."

Clough, however, had other ideas. Martin O'Neill and Frank Clark were also trying to work off injuries and on the morning of the match Clough sat his players down on the perimeter of the Olympic Stadium pitch - within a few yards of the spot where John Robertson would cross the ball for Trevor Francis's decisive goal later that day.

Squatting on a football, Clough turned to O'Neill first. "Young man, I'd like to know if you think you are fit?"

"Right as rain, Gaffer," replied the Irishman.

Clark echoed O'Neill and then it was Gemmill's turn. "Sure, boss, I can play. Absolutely perfect."

Clough had already prepared his response. "Smashing. I'm delighted. So everybody's fit and everyone can play."

His voice grew louder. "Well I for one think you're all lying and I can risk only one of you." He pointed at Clark. "You play, Frank."

O'Neill, never usually short of a word or two, somehow managed to seethe in silence but Gemmill could not contain the vitriol. First there were a few seconds of silence, as if he was trying to digest what he was hearing. Then he rose to his feet. "Well, fuck you," he shouted, launching into a tirade that would have serious repercussions for his future at the club.

In hindsight he wishes that he had been able to emulate O'Neill's restraint, but his reaction was of a man who believed Clough had reneged on a gentleman's agreement. "I'd been promised that if I proved my fitness I was playing. I'd played in every match up to the semi-final and as far as I was concerned I was fine. So I made sure I had my say. I exploded, to be honest. I was carrying on and on and in the end the boss had to tell me to get a grip.

# ARCHIE GEMMILL

"It was a terrible experience, truly dreadful. Everyone has such great memories of that night but I have to be honest and I hated every minute of it. Every second of every minute.

"I was lucky enough to have a good career and achieve most of my ambitions. I won three league titles, the League Cup, I captained my country and I played in the World Cup. But every footballer wants to play in the biggest club game there is, and that's the European Cup final. So I sat on the bench that night absolutely spewing, and I don't feel too much better talking about it now. Honestly, I cannot forget it.

"I couldn't even bring myself to join in the celebrations. They kept a medal for me but I just went straight back down the tunnel. Look at the photographs - I'm not on any of them. I wasn't even there when they went up to get the trophy."

Clark remembers that out of the three players he was the least likely to be selected. "I was certainly not 100 per cent, whereas Martin and Archie were adamant about their fitness. I was delighted but the two of them were devastated - I mean, out of it, bitter. I asked Brian afterwards why he had chosen me and he said: 'I was less likely to disbelieve you.' Basically his decision said: 'I can't trust you, Martin, or you, Archie, but I can trust you, Frank.' It was Clough's instinct."

The decision to leave out O'Neill was justified to some extent when a week later his hamstring went again while playing for Northern Ireland in Copenhagen. Yet Gemmill maintains to this day that he was adequately fit. The pain was so acute, the wound so deep, that the scars remain.

"I wasn't worried about Martin's feelings, I just cared about myself. I'm 'mardy' - that's the word, isn't it? People would try to cheer me up by telling me 'there's always next year.' Sure enough, Forest reached the final the following year but by then I was long gone. Martin got his medal after all, but in the summer after the first final they [Clough and Taylor] showed me who was boss and sold me to Birmingham. They thought I'd overstepped the mark because of what I'd said to them. It was a serious falling-out and a lot of things were said."

So did he regret it? "Maybe, maybe not. Some people stand up for themselves more than others. It's got me in trouble on more than one occasion but you've got to go with your gut feeling, and if you feel you're being badly treated you have every entitlement to speak up.

"That was my version of events anyway but Pete called me into the office before the start of the next season. 'Archie, you're finished here,' he told me. They wanted me on my way, as simple as that."

Gemmill will always maintain he was jettisoned as a direct consequence of his stream of invective in Munich. Clough, however, used to say it was because he was trying to reduce the age of the squad.

Whatever the truth (and it probably lies somewhere in between) Forest's loss was Birmingham's gain. Jim Smith, Birmingham's manager at the time, remembers Gemmill as being the pivotal figure in a team that immediately won promotion to the First Division. "I have never seen a player on the pitch, or even during training, who had so much desire to win," says Smith. "He worked himself and those around him, especially the younger ones, to the limit."

Clough and Taylor had bought Asa Hartford to replace Gemmill, but within a matter of weeks they were acknowledging their blunder and 63 days after arriving in Nottingham he was sold to Everton. To make matters worse, Hartford had cost £500,000 from Manchester City, more than three times the amount Birmingham paid for Gemmill. Forest recouped most of their money but it will still go down as one of Clough's biggest aberrations. "It was a mistake on my part," he says in his autobiography. "I thought his [Gemmill's] legs had gone but he proved that I should have kept him on for at least another year."

Taylor also regretted it, even if he never admitted as much in public, although he would go on to work with Gemmill again when he split from Clough and was appointed as Derby's manager. Together, they masterminded one of Clough's darkest hours, when Gemmill scored in a 2-0 defeat of Forest in the FA Cup third round at the Baseball Ground in 1983.

"Archie was a strange mixture," Taylor wrote in *With Clough By Taylor*. "A hard man, yet he would blush at a compliment. A tiger on the pitch and a lamb off it. A loyal friend yet a born moaner nicknamed 'The Nark.' He was a perfectionist, striving always for a flawless performance, so he was irritated by my insistence: 'You can't deliver the ball.' It was largely true; I didn't say it just to get a rise out of him. Passing was the only weakness in his game, but how he worked to improve on it."

"Brian always said he wished he had never sold me," says Gemmill. "Well, I wished the same. I still had a year left on my contract, I'd started pre-season and all I was thinking about was getting back in the team. I could have dug my heels in but once you're told you're no longer welcome you might as well go. I had no choice really, but it's strange to think I did not even last two years at Forest. People talk about me as if I was part of the furniture at the City Ground, but I played only 80 games."

The acrimonious circumstances behind his departure were largely forgotten in later years but it was a thoroughly unsatisfactory way for Gemmill to end his playing days under Clough and Taylor, an association stretching back to 1970 when Derby signed the Scotland under-23 international and former St Mirren player from Third Division Preston.

It would be another eight years before Gemmill was reunited with Clough and this time it was in a coaching capacity. Initially he was put in charge of the youth team and when Liam O'Kane became the first-team coach Gemmill was given responsibility for the reserve team as well.

In six seasons they won the reserve league three times and finished runners-up three times although, without doubt, Gemmill's greatest achievement from this stage of his career was in the development of so many talented young players. The seemingly endless conveyor belt threw up, among others, Steve Stone, Mark Crossley, Terry Wilson, Darren Wassall, Gary Charles, Lee Glover and Steve Chettle. Gemmill also nurtured his son Scot, who went on to make 288 appearances for the club as well as going to the 1998 World Cup finals with Scotland and winning 26 international caps. His appointment coincided with the emergence of a side that grew to regard Wembley as an annual part of the fixture list, with six visits in four seasons. For a while it seemed as though Clough could do no wrong, but Gemmill was also there to see his downfall, a story of relegation, worrying illness and a reliance on alcohol.

The beginning of the end could probably be traced back to Clough's decision to send out Gemmill, O'Kane and the physiotherapist Graham Lyas to rouse the players before extra-time in the 1991 FA Cup final against Tottenham.

While Terry Venables trotted on to the pitch to exert his influence on his own players, Clough sat impassively on the bench beside Ron Fenton. "I certainly wasn't expecting it," says Gemmill. "He was quite matter of fact - he wasn't getting out of his seat and it was up to us to lift the players. But I'm never going to criticise him. People were queuing up to analyse what he had done wrong but if Des Walker hadn't scored an own goal and Forest had won that match it would have been described as a masterstroke."

Yet the FA Cup *did* slip through Clough's fingers. We will never know if that Wembley disappointment was directly linked to his decline in health, but one certainty is that his intake of alcohol escalated over the next two years, culminating in his botched retirement and the team's demotion in the inaugural Premiership season.

"That last season was difficult for everybody, but particularly for the manager," recalls Gemmill. "He had problems with drink that were getting the better of him. It's just sad that it ended that way because it must have a terrible time for him, watching it all slip away, and his family must have suffered as well.

"But I have to say that once he had his liver transplant and gave up his drinking he always seemed to be in terrific health. I would go to his house for a cup of tea and a biscuit and we would have a general chat about life. And I can assure you that until the day he died he was as sharp as a tack.

"He could talk about politics all night along. You could put him in any situation in the world and he would stand his ground and inevitably come out a winner.

"They say that if you drink too much you start losing some of your brain cells. Well, he could go back to his playing days at

Middlesbrough and Sunderland and tell you the names of all his teammates, where they lived, what age they were. Then he would start talking about all the great games at Derby and Forest and his memory for detail was unbelievable. I just hope he enjoyed those afternoons we spent together as much as I did."

Occasionally they would bicker about the rights and wrongs of leaving him out of the team in Munich. Or, when he was feeling particularly mischievous, Gemmill would remind Clough of the FA Cup goal he scored against Forest.

"Nearly always, though, he would have the last word. In fact, it was probably always. Remember that television interview? The one where he said if he had any problems with his players he would sit them down, discuss it for 20 minutes and then they would decide he was right. Well, that was the boss in a nutshell.

"We'd reminisce about the old days and invariably the subject of the European Cup final would come up. I would try to tell him why he was in the wrong. And he would say: 'What was the score again?' You could talk until you were blue in the face but at the end of the day there was going to be only person who was right - and that was him."

Gemmill's brief dalliance with management at Rotherham - 29 wins in 93 games - was a chastening experience, but his eye for young talent has subsequently led to Derby employing him as their European scout and the Scottish Football Association asking him to take charge of their under-19s team.

He does not come across as a nostalgic type and it is noticeable that, of all the Forest players from the glory years, he is rarely seen doing interviews. Yet he has clearly retained his affection for the club. "Even now, whenever I go back I get treated brilliantly," he says.

Before heading home he makes a point of asking for a copy of the finished book but the interview ends as it starts - on a low point. "You're chapter 12," I tell him.

"Oh, Jesus!" he says. "Substitute again."

# THIRTEEN

# Roy Keane

*He's 19 and doesn't know where his talent comes from. Nobody does. It's just there.*

**Brian Clough**

WHEN ROY KEANE was 16 he wrote to every club in England asking for a trial. One by one the rejections began to drop through the letterbox at 88 Ballinderry Park, Mayfield, Cork. "As I am sure you will appreciate, we receive literally hundreds of similar letters each week," began the one with the Nottingham postmark. "As it is usual to favour letters from players who have representative honours, or ones who are highly recommended by someone close to football, I regret that we are unable to offer you a trial."

How typical of Keane that he still has that letter. And how fortuitous for Forest that nobody else snapped him up. Keane went unnoticed, like a gem at the bottom of the Irish sea, for another two years before a Forest scout, Noel McCabe, told his employers to "get this kid to England" before some other club found out about him.

His first match was at Liverpool on August 28th, 1990. "Nobody knew who he was," says Brian Laws. "Cloughie used to bring young kids along to put out the kit. Cloughie said: 'Roy, go and put that shirt on, see what it's like'.

"Roy put it on and Cloughie said: 'Roy, you look fantastic. Tell you what, keep it on, you're playing'. We started laughing, thinking Cloughie was taking the mickey out of this kid. Cloughie said: 'No, he's playing - Lawsy look after him, he's playing right midfield.'"

"I went to him and said: 'What's your name, son?'
'Roy'.

'Listen, Roy, I will try to help you as much as I can'.

"But there was no fear in him. John Barnes was playing left wing for Liverpool and Roy kicked seven bells out of him.

"Barnes turned to Roy and said: 'Who the hell do you think you are?'

'Fuck off,' said Keane.

"I thought to myself: 'He's going to be a star'."

It was an amazingly steep learning curve but Keane was an excellent student.

In his first home match Keane made such a favourable impression against Southampton the crowd gave him a standing ovation when he was substituted with the score at 3-1.

Four weeks later he had his first experience of playing at Old Trafford. "The game kicked off, the ball went back to Bryan Robson and Roy absolutely creamed him," recalls Sir Alex Ferguson. "I thought: "Bloody cheek of him - how dare he come to Old Trafford and tackle Robbo like that! I made a mental note there and then that we had to get this boy to Old Trafford."

Keane was not just strong in the challenge but tremendous in the air and, for one so slight, blessed with extraordinary stamina. He had anticipation, courage, a fine shot and immaculate control and, without fear of exaggeration, his muddy heroism in the League Cup semi-final at Tottenham in 1992 (scoring the extra-time winner with an unstoppable header) ranks as one of the outstanding individual displays of any Forest player ever.

He was never the firebrand that he became at Manchester United but even in the early days Keane was a sleeves-up motivator who could inspire his team-mates and single-handedly lift the crowd.

He was never quicker to speak than when he felt someone around him was giving less than his best. And as hard as he was on his teammates, he was always far more unforgiving of himself.

As Laws says: "It didn't matter whether he was earning £5 or £5,000 a week, you knew with Roy he would give you everything." Coming from a council estate in a city reeling from its Ford and Dunlop factory closures, Keane had faced a lifetime of unemployment or low-paid labouring until Forest added him to their payroll. In his mind, he owed the club everything. And he was smart enough to understand that a disciplinarian such as Clough would knock some of the rougher adolescent edges off him.

He was "delighted to oblige" when he found Clough waiting for him one morning, holding his muddy trainers after walking Dell, his golden retriever, and wanting them cleaned.

Nor did he complain when he scored the winning goal in an FA Cup quarter-final at Norwich in 1991 and Clough threatened to sell him to the circus for celebrating with a forward somersault.

Clough even resorted to violence to teach Keane a lesson after a third-round replay at home to Crystal Palace that same season. Forest were winning 2-1, courtesy of goals from Terry Wilson and Stuart Pearce, when Keane under-hit a back-pass, forcing Mark Crossley to rush from his penalty area and punt the ball clear. It went straight to John Salako who chipped the ball into the empty goal from 50 yards. When Keane trudged back into the dressing room Clough floored him with a punch to the jaw.

"Don't pass the ball back to the goalkeeper," he screamed, as Keane lay sprawled out on the floor.

Clough's hard-line discipline worked in the respect that Keane was never sent off at Forest, whereas he has served 29 matches in suspensions since moving to Manchester United. But it would be exaggerating to say he was an angel in Nottingham - or anything like one.

He seemed to lead a dual life at times. He had a beautiful house in Scarrington, a picturesque village famous locally for the 17ft-high pile of thousands of horseshoes outside the old smithy. His neighbours remember him as quiet and unassuming, and Ian Storey-Moore, who was the landlord of The Wheatsheaf in nearby Bingham, describes him as "a great lad and never any bother."

But then there were stories of Keane punching and puking his way through the city's nightspots.

"I barred him from my pub," says Larry Lloyd, once the landlord of The Stage Door on Upper Parliament Street. "It was Christmas and Stuart Pearce had asked me if he could bring the lads in for an afternoon drink. This was before all-day licensing hours, but I was happy to draw the curtains and lock the doors. But when it got to normal evening opening hours Keane was jumping up and down on the tables, shouting his mouth off and acting the fool. I had to pull him down by his coat.

"He was horrible when he had a drink. I gave him short shrift at my place but he used to get in all sorts of trouble elsewhere. The bouncers at the Black Orchid would end up slapping him every week. But it seemed to me that he was looking for trouble rather than it finding him."

With success on the field came trouble off it, and there were times, by his own admission, when Keane seemed intent on living like one of the Gallagher brothers. He was arrested, thrown out of nightclubs and had his nose bloodied. Clough sent him home from a trip to Jersey after he poured a pint of lager over a woman hockey player.

"He made a few mistakes off the pitch," says Alan Hill, then Forest's chief scout. "He was just the typical lad about town. If you're a genius as a football player you can become a little arrogant and Roy was no different.

"We had to bring him into line a few times but it would be wrong to concentrate on his bad points. I did a television interview a while back and spoke for two hours about what a great player he was. But I also gave them an anecdote about one of his nights out and, guess what, that was the only bit they showed. Roy phoned me up and he was ever so annoyed. I said: 'Did you see the full interview?' He said: 'No, but I saw the bit that went out.' He holds things like that against you."

Hill has not forgotten the surge of exhilaration he felt the first time he saw Keane in action. "He was always so focused. He had had a lot of knock-backs from clubs when he was younger and it was as if he was determined from day one to prove everyone wrong.

"He was as shy as anything back then and didn't dare say a word to anyone. At Manchester United he has this image of being unapproachable but it was nothing like that. I can still remember how white he went when Cloughie told him he was playing at Anfield. The gaffer put his arm round him and gave him a kiss on the cheek but he was as pale as a ghost. But he was brilliant that night and he's been like that ever since. It was a pleasure to work with him. I still talk to him every now and then but I'm like everybody else - I haven't got his number."

He left, of course - like all Forest's best players seem to. But, parochialism aside, who could really say he should have hugged the shores when the high seas offered so many new adventures? Forest had just been relegated and Keane would have been a fool to decline the opportunity to stand at the summit of his profession and find out exactly how good he really was.

When he returned to the City Ground in United's colours two seasons later the atmosphere was caustic, bitter and, all in all, thoroughly unfair. Keane had cost Forest a bargain-of-the-century £47,000 from Cobh Ramblers, he had played 154 games, scored 33 goals from midfield and the club had sold him for £3.75m, then a British record.

Perhaps the abuse was just inevitable. Watching one of your heroes leave for another club can feel like being dumped by your first girlfriend. And when Manchester United are that club it feels like losing out to the coolest boy at school, the one who got all the girls and wore the best clothes.

Yet many of those fans spewing vitriol in his direction were the same people who voted him their player-of-the-year in the 1992/93 relegation season. Maybe, just maybe, he would have been granted a better reception if the hecklers had known of his disgust when certain teammates were cracking jokes in the showers after Forest's fate had been sealed. We will never know, of course, but if everyone had shared Keane's dedication Forest would surely never have gone down.

As Clough wrote in *Walking on Water*: "Keane was the genuine article. I never remember him giving an ounce less than his utmost, his absolute maximum, in a Forest shirt."

Getting to Keane, however, is like asking for breakfast with the Pope. He is unwilling to be interviewed, for reasons he will not divulge, and his agent's sombre tone indicates that once he has made up his mind only the most savage form of Victorian torture could persuade him otherwise.

Undaunted, I make a second request, this time via Manchester United's press office. A few days later I get an email back. "We have spoken to Roy and unfortunately this is not something he is able to do, purely due to prior commitments."

I am not totally surprised. A few years ago, en route to a press conference, I had been driving along the tiny country road leading towards Manchester United's training ground when his silver Mercedes was coming the other way.

Would he move over?

Would he hell. I was almost in the ditch by the time he leant out of his window and started screaming at this "fecking idiot." The malevolence of his rage was frightening. For one dreadful moment I knew how C. Thomas Howell's character must have felt as he stared into Rutger Hauer's eyes in *The Hitcher*.

I wrote about it, of course, comparing him to that other temperamental, boozy Irishman, Father Jack Hackett. And it might not have been a total coincidence that Alfie Haaland, nursing a bad knee and an even worse grudge, chose me for his first interview to discuss his infamous feud with Keane.

So, it was not a huge shock to find Keane, that notorious grudge-bearer, being so elusive.

In his autobiography he states "the City Ground and the Forest fans will always have a special place in my heart." But it is a long time ago now, and Keane has always been a man who seems defiantly free of sentimentality. Somehow I cannot imagine him rushing into the dressing room after matches at Old Trafford to check the Forest result. Or that he ever picked out Andy Reid on Republic of Ireland trips to get the latest gossip from his old club.

It is a pity, however, that he cannot juggle around some of those "prior commitments". It would be interesting to find out how Clough's death had affected him. He could have gone into detail about some of those nights out with Des Walker and what exactly he had said to Justin Edinburgh and Steve Sedgley in the 1991 FA Cup final.

I get the feeling he is a far more intelligent character than the psychotic image that is sometimes portrayed. He is not a monster. Not all of the time, anyway.

Everyone knows the cold, detached, grudging Keane. Not many people know the story of how, just after leaving Forest, he visited a young boy in a Cork hospital who was stricken with cancer and had not long to live. Keane spent hours at his bedside and gave him one of his Irish football jerseys. He made such an impression the youngster was buried in Keane's shirt.

Equally, Keane made a point of being among the mourners at Clough's memorial service in Derby, driving from Manchester on a filthy October night. Keane, it should be noted, had missed a Champions League match the previous night because of flu and presumably went against his doctor's orders to take his place at Pride Park.

The truth probably is that no one knows the real Keane, apart from his family and a handful of mates back at the Temple Acre Tavern in Cork. And that is the way he likes it. After years of nightclub spats and other dubious nocturnal sprees, these days he rooms by himself, reads by himself and keeps to himself.

When Mick McCarthy was Ireland's manager Keane was considered so unapproachable the rest of the squad often had to make contingency plans for routine tasks such as autographing shirts and footballs. Nobody, quite simply, would dare risk disturbing the captain and, besides, the kit-man Johnny Fallon had perfected a fine Keane signature.

As Niall Quinn recalls: "Getting the kit-man to forge the signature of one of your teammates is the price you pay for accommodating genius."

That genius was not at Forest long, but we should be eternally grateful that it all began at the City Ground.

# FOURTEEN

# John Robertson

*If ever I felt off colour I'd sit next to him,
because compared with this fat, dumpy lad I was Errol
Flynn. But give him a ball and a yard of grass and he was
an artist - the Picasso of our game.*

**Brian Clough**

AND THEN THERE was one. John Neilson Robertson: officially the best player in Nottingham Forest's history. A man who polled even higher than Stuart Pearce when fans voted for their favourite all-time team in 1998. Only three people declined to include Robertson, and what planet were they on? He was the talisman. The inspiration. If he had fallen into the River Trent he would have come up with a salmon in his mouth.

He had my vote too - helped by the fact that, during his days as the landlord of the Greyhound in Aslockton, he served me my first pint. Under-age, of course, but my sixth-form stubble and fake ID seemed to deceive him.

In those days Robertson could usually be found perched behind the lounge bar, wheezing with laughter and reeking of fags. It was difficult at times, looking at this walking plume of smoke, to remember this was the man who set up the decisive goal in one European Cup final and scored the winner himself the following year. A player so gifted he could land the ball in a waste-paper basket from 40 yards. Without touching the sides.

Yet Robertson's charm has always been that he was an unlikely hero. In his early years the stovies-loving Scot seemed more interested in Roxy Music, even copying Bryan Ferry's haircut, than a top-flight career in football. "I'll admit I did have a chip on my shoulder at one stage," he says. He feasted on too much fast-food, smoked too many cigarettes and, according to Brian Clough, was hovering on the brink of failure as a professional footballer.

Certainly Clough could never have imagined his "little fat lad" would not only become Forest's best player but one day take charge of Glasgow Celtic, alongside Martin O'Neill, as one half of the most supreme managerial partnership in British football since, well, Brian Clough and Peter Taylor. Robertson even looks quite dapper as he leads me through a labyrinth of corridors inside Celtic Park, chirpily informing the first-team coach Steve Walford about the Nottingham vote ("don't tell Martin," came the reply) before plonking himself down in a chair in the players' games room. There is no potbelly, no double chin and, all in all, Robertson has aged well considering that, back in his heyday, even getting on the team coach seemed an arduous task.

"He didn't jump on with the air or surefootedness of an athlete," Clough wrote in *Walking on Water*. "He waddled up to it, put his left foot first on the bottom step and was the only player to use the handrails to help himself through the door. Oh yeah, and you'd occasionally see him squash his fag under his other foot."

Robertson held his cigarette Mafioso-style, with the end pointing into the palm of his hand, so Clough would not see it. He would skulk inside the entrance to the Jubilee Club, hiding behind a rubber plant, while sympathetic teammates created a diversion outside. But however much he guzzled Polo mints and scrubbed the nicotine stains from his fingers, he was invariably given away by the stench of cigarette smoke on his clothes. "A slob - an absolute slob," Clough concluded.

Clough's first impressions were of a "scruffy, unfit, uninterested waste of time" - a man whose lifestyle could have been the inspiration behind Norm Peterson's character in *Cheers*. Or Rab C. Nesbitt. He accused Robertson of living out of a frying pan, and said he ought to take the words "professional footballer" off his passport.

Taylor went even further, throwing Robertson off the practice pitch, by way of introduction, on a pre-season visit to West Germany in 1976. "Almost my first words to him were: 'You're a disgrace and ought to be sent home'," Taylor wrote in *With Clough By Taylor*, recalling that Robertson's warm-up routine consisted of "not moving out of a five-yard radius throughout the entire quarter of an hour."

"Talk about rude awakenings," smiles Robertson. "That was the first time I'd actually met him. We were all sat on the grass for a team meeting and he picked me out: 'You - sod off back to the hotel.'

"I couldn't believe it. 'What have I done? What have I done?' I kept saying.

"He said: 'Never you mind - I'll see you later. And it might save time if you start packing now'."

Back at the hotel Taylor caught up with Robertson by the swimming pool, with "a spare tyre bulging over his trunks."

He did not mince his words. "It was an almighty dressing down," says Robertson. "Basically, he told me I'd fallen in the gutter and that I had to climb out or ship out. But it was constructive criticism. Okay, he'd deliberately showed me up in front of my mates - but it was all done for a reason. He said he wouldn't have done it if he didn't think that deep down I could be a good player. We had a good chat and the message got through.

"I'd already had it from Clough - more than once - and it was the boot up the backside I needed. Before Clough arrived I was on the transfer list and, if I'm being brutally honest, I'd begun to feel the whole world was against me.

"Allan Brown [Clough's predecessor] didn't think I worked hard enough and he even tried to pack me off back to Scotland. They fancied a lad at Partick Thistle called Ronnie Glaven and Brown asked me if I wanted to be part of the deal. I told him I'd think about it - but there was no way I was ever going to say yes.

"Because of all that, I'd got into the stage of feeling sorry for myself and, appearance-wise, I'd started letting myself go. I don't want to spoil the myth but I was never as bad a smoker as people said I was. But I probably felt everyone was against me and I would slouch around the dressing room, thinking how unfortunate I was. They looked at me and decided they didn't like my attitude - and I don't blame them."

# DEEP INTO THE FOREST

Even by Clough's record of turning base metal into gold, there was something remarkable about Robertson's metamorphosis from under-motivated midfielder to one of the most bewitching wingers in the world. He was never an orthodox wide man, someone who found it an irresistible personal challenge to dribble past his marker. Yet his ability to cross the ball under pressure was peerless. He needed only half a yard to whip over a tantalising centre and could deliver the ball perfectly with either foot.

Slowly but surely, and to the intense frustration of the right-sided O'Neill, Forest became a team that instinctively looked left. "Just give it to Robbo," was the cry.

Robertson was the Second Division's player-of-the-year when Forest won promotion in 1976/77, and he wasted little time in announcing himself as an exceptional performer at the highest level. As Forest swept to the top of the old First Division he started to play with the guile and wit to trouble the most accomplished defender. It was as if he was on first-name terms with the ball.

In November 1977 the esteemed James Lawton wrote in the *Express*: "Is Nottingham Forest's runaway leadership of the First Division all to do with Brian Clough's talent for striding across the otherwise troubled waters of English soccer? Or is it because the majority of their rivals have yet to show the gumption required to identify the source of Forest's strength - and the basic know-how to deal with it?

"Forest scored 17 goals against two last month and even a casual observer could note that their pale-faced, dark-haired 24-year-old Scottish winger John Robertson was the man at the heart of it all. Whether he is dawdling in a deep position down the left wing, driving either side of his shadow or delivering balls of deep penetration early or late, he is clearly the man who matters."

Robertson is too modest to accept as much, but his colleagues have never been in any doubt. "He was the star," volunteers Garry Birtles. "I played with some great players in my time - Bryan Robson, Tony Woodcock, Peter Shilton, to name but three - but he was just different class. Liverpool used to double-mark him with Phil Neal and Jimmy Case and the slippery little sod still found a way out. That first five yards, he just got away. And he was a better crosser of the ball than David Beckham. Sheer class."

"The little fat bastard was a magician," adds Larry Lloyd, in his inimitable style. "He was slower than me but he had the first two yards on anybody because his brain was quicker than everybody else. You ask him to run from the halfway line to the corner flag and every other player on the field would beat him. He was the slowest runner in the world but he had that extra two yards. He'd put his fat arse one way, the defender would go that way, 30,000 people would go that way as well, and he was the only person going the other way with the ball. See you later!

"I don't think he realised how good he actually was. And the main thing with Robbo: there was an end product. Not only would he cross the ball accurately, he would do it so the little 'dickie' where you pumped it up was turned the other way so you didn't hurt your head."

Robertson was brought up in Uddingston on the south-eastern tip of Glasgow and played for the same youth team, Drumchapel Amateurs, where Sir Alex Ferguson and David Moyes began their careers. The Hosier Secondary pupil became a regular fixture in the Scotland schoolboys' team, catching the eye of Forest's then assistant manager Bill Anderson, who drove to Glasgow in 1968 and persuaded the teenager's parents to allow him to come south.

To begin with, Robertson was miserable with homesickness. "I was only 15 and for the first three or four months it was really unsettling," he says. "But once we all got together at the youth hostel - Dave Serella, Jimmy McCann and a few others - I grew to love Nottingham. I've still got my house there and when I'm finished in Glasgow I'll be moving back."

Matt Gillies awarded him his debut, aged 17, in a 3-1 defeat of Blackpool in October 1970 and, having cleaned Duncan McKenzie's boots for the previous 18 months, Robertson began to establish himself as a first-team player in the 1971/72 season.

It was a desperately difficult period in which to make a mark, with Ian Storey-Moore leaving for Manchester United and the subsequent downward spiral culminating in relegation to the Second Division.

# DEEP INTO THE FOREST

In October 1972 Gillies was replaced by Dave Mackay, who recognised Robertson's ability and gave him an extended run in central midfield. "He was great for me - and Martin O'Neill, for that matter," says Robertson. "But just as I was beginning to do well I injured my knee in a friendly against Benfica at the Stadium of Light. By the time I regained fitness, Mackay had left to take Brian Clough's place at Derby.

"Allan Brown came in but he put me off on his very first day. I'd played about 30 games that year and in our very first conversation he called me 'Jimmy'. I mean, who the bloody hell is Jimmy?"

So it was that Robertson's big adventure south had turned sour by the time Hurricane Clough blew into Nottingham in January 1975. "I can remember his first day so vividly. I was sat in the dressing room facing the doors and, bang, suddenly they swung open. What I really remember is the way he strode in. He was so purposeful. He took his jacket off and in one movement flung it on a peg. I don't even know how he knew the peg was there. I remember thinking: 'Jesus, he means business, this guy.'

"You could feel this incredible electricity. He set to work immediately, put the journalists in the trophy room and told us we were going for training. There were no pleasantries, no introductions, no shaking hands. After that everyone bucked up their ideas. We had no choice."

Robertson had been a disaffected fringe player under his previous three managers, and it took Clough longer than many people realise to spot the classic wingers' gifts of skill and swerve.

"I got my lucky break in an FA Cup tie against Fulham because Paul Richardson was suspended. I didn't realise it at the time but it was John Lawson [the Nottingham Evening Post's Forest correspondent] who put my name forward. Clough didn't really know much about me so he'd asked the local paper guy and he suggested that I was worth a look."

The transition to left-wing did not occur until a pre-season tour of Northern Ireland seven months into Clough's tenure. Robertson's initial reluctance was eased by the knowledge that he was at least in the team and he responded by having a hand in all three Forest goals in a 3-2 win against Coleraine.

# JOHN ROBERTSON

From that moment the historic haunt of Stuart Imlach, "Flip" Le Flem and Ian Storey-Moore was now home to a stooped, jinking magician whose sleight of foot and nonchalant half-walk, half-run would illuminate the City Ground for the next six seasons.

"I felt at home straight away. I'd played on the left for Scotland schoolboys so I knew the position, but when I first came to Forest I had seen myself playing in the middle. It was two years after the World Cup, Alf Ramsey's 'wingless wonders' and all that, and nobody really seemed to like wingers back then."

It helped that Robertson was that rare commodity - a genuinely two-footed player who was equally at ease whichever side he went.

"Real Madrid were my childhood heroes and I used to fancy myself as the next Ferenc Puskas. As a wee boy I told myself I would have to be able to kick it with my left if I really wanted to be like him. So I would spend hours kicking the ball against a fence.

"Then my brother, Hughie, would come out and we would play this game where he stood 20 yards away and I had to hit him with the ball, kicking with my left. 'Don't make me move,' he would shout. The funny thing is that in later years some people actually thought I was left-footed, although it should have given the game away that I took penalties with my right."

Anyone who doubts Robertson was the vital cog in Forest's machinery need only look at a montage of video clips of that period from 1977 to 1980, when Forest greedily accumulated just about every undefeated and sequential record that was going. Robertson did not miss a single match in the first three seasons back in the top division. He scored the decisive penalty to win the replayed 1978 League Cup final against Liverpool. There was his diving header in the first leg of the European Cup semi-final against Cologne, playing despite the death of his brother in a car crash the previous Saturday. There were the countless occasions when he would stylishly pick out a Forest attacker inside the six-yard area, not least Trevor Francis in the 1979 European Cup final against Malmo. And there was his sheer gall to walk out at Anfield at the height of the Forest-Liverpool rivalry and playfully pretend to take a penalty in front of the Kop. Robertson was not just the doyen of wing-play but the penalty king - and he knew it. In the championship season he converted no fewer than nine successful spot-kicks.

"Winning the European Cups was an absolutely unbelievable feeling but, believe me, the players took as much joy from winning the league," he says. "Nobody took it seriously when we first went to the top of the table. Then we went to Manchester United and absolutely murdered them 4-0. We'd been turning over teams at home but that day everything just clicked. We knew after that we had arrived. We went to Benidorm and John O'Hare, whose opinion everyone respected, told us we had a great chance. And we just kept on winning."

When the subject turns to Forest's exploits on the Continent Robertson is happy to confirm he was irked by Barry Davies's commentary for the winning goal against Malmo. "Maybe it shouldn't but, yeah, that really bugged me. I got the cross in for Trevor Francis to score but when I saw it replayed on television Barry Davies made some clever remark that he'd been waiting all night for me to do that. Now, every time that goal is shown on television, that's what you hear. Well, sorry, but opposition teams aren't stupid. You can't go on a football field and do exactly what you want as easily as that, especially in a European Cup final. Malmo had been showing me inside all night. They'd done their homework. That was the first opportunity they had given me to go wide."

The fact that Forest's achievements are frequently overlooked by the media also rankles. "We won it two years running. Twice! When you look back at that era only Liverpool won the European Cup more times than us. Manchester United have done it twice - but with two different sides over a period of 30 years. Barcelona have done it once. Arsenal? Chelsea? They would love to say they ruled Europe like we did. Doesn't that say it all? And look where Forest came from, languishing towards the bottom of the old Second Division.

"If we'd been a big-city club everyone would have been waxing lyrical about us. Instead, all we ever heard about was 'journeymen' and a 'ragtag and bobtail team.' Well, you don't win what we won without being highly talented footballers, every last one of us. We had one of the greatest goalkeepers ever, for starters, and two centre-halves who would never let anybody go by. We had character, pace and steel and, quite simply, I don't think we ever got the credit we deserved. For a club the size of Forest to achieve what we achieved, I think people should look back and feel a real sense of pride. It was monumental. I can't see it ever happening again."

It is doubtful too that Forest will ever see a winger of such consistent talent again. In the years since Robertson left the City Ground the left-wing position became known in the dressing room as "the graveyard." The closest there has been is Andy Reid, the talented Dubliner who emerged as the outstanding player under Paul Hart's management and immediately drew comparisons with Robertson. Yet Reid, for all his skill, is not two-footed and his reputation was forged at places such as Bramall Lane and Gresty Road, rather than against the toughest sides in Europe.

Even when sides man-marked Robertson he would usually find a way of getting through. "We tried it before the European Cup final," says Bobby Houghton, the former Malmo coach who later became Dave Bassett's assistant at the City Ground in the late-90s. "It didn't matter. Some players would run around and try to shake off their marker. Not Robertson. He just stayed where he was and waited for the ball. He knew he needed only a yard or two to get his crosses in and that's exactly how it turned out."

In one spell Houghton's players fouled Robertson no fewer than five times in three minutes. It was not that the Swedes were a cynical team - just that Robertson could induce panic every time he was in possession of the ball.

"John always had outstanding ability," says Viv Anderson, reminiscing about their days pre-Clough. "I can remember when we were in the reserves we used to play five-a-side matches in a small courtyard. One game he nutmegged me about 50 times. Usually you would say that was a fluke but he did it so often it must have been more than that.

"He was lazy and he had always been podgy because, as Clough and Taylor kept on reminding everyone, he liked his chips. He was a unique player. I mean, there aren't many fat and slow left-wingers about."

# DEEP INTO THE FOREST

In Robertson's testimonial programme - "There's only one JR" - there are equally lavish tributes from, among others, Bill Shankly, Jock Stein, Ron Greenwood, Graeme Souness and Kenny Dalglish.

Peter Taylor wrote: "Over the years I've seen any number of left-wingers, including the likes of Gento, the famous Real Madrid player who everyone used to rave about. Well, you can have the lot for me - in terms of productivity nobody compares with John."

Jimmy Gordon, the then Forest trainer, paid Robertson the ultimate compliment. "I saw a lot of Tom Finney and Stan Matthews in my time and it was very difficult to choose between them. But when you look at what Finney and Matthews had to offer, John has a bit of both ... and something extra on top."

Robertson's benefit match, a scoreless draw against Leicester City in May 1980, was infamous for Stan Bowles taking offence when he was left out of the side and quitting the club. But that paled into insignificance compared to the manner of Robertson's own departure three years later.

"I'd rather forget about that now - I made a terrible mistake," Robertson says of his notorious and hugely divisive move to Derby, a transfer that acted as the final blow in the deteriorating relationship between Clough and Taylor.

To condense a tortuous, sometimes torturous, saga into a few paragraphs, Robertson had been nearing the end of his contract at the City Ground and Taylor, then the Derby manager, capitalised by offering him a deal. Clough was away on a charity walk, oblivious to everything, when he received a telephone call telling him his favourite player had abandoned him.

Crucially, neither Robertson nor Taylor had even phoned Clough, an act of discourtesy he regarded as treacherous disloyalty."Like I say, it was a mistake - a dreadful error," says Robertson. "If I could turn back time - and I would love to - I would never have done it .All I can say is that I started to believe my own publicity. I started to think I could go anywhere and be a success."

Not at Derby, however. Clough, never more dangerous than when he had a genuine grievance, revealed offers from Luton and

# JOHN ROBERTSON

Southampton at a transfer tribunal, bumping up Robertson's price to £135,000, far higher than Derby had expected to pay. The upshot was that they could not afford to strengthen other areas of the team and Taylor was sacked as they were relegated to the Second Division.

For nearly two years there was an unofficial ban on Robertson showing his face at the City Ground. But it spoke volumes for Clough's regard for Robertson that he finally waived his own sanctions to bring him back in August 1985.

"Sadly, things were never the same," reflects Robertson. He had family problems and "football wasn't utmost in my world at that stage." He played only 12 games before leaving for non-league Corby Town, simultaneously moving into the pub trade.

After a total 514 appearances for the club, 95 goals and 26 Scotland international caps, incorporating the 1978 World Cup in Argentina and a Wembley winner against England ("still my proudest moment"), Robertson remained a welcome visitor to the ground - although his enduring popularity did not spare him from the occasional Clough tirade.

Ian Edwards, formerly the *Nottingham Evening Post*'s Forest correspondent, remembers standing with Robertson outside the Jubilee Club one September morning in 1990, when Clough suddenly bounded across the car park.

"The previous night Forest had beaten Burnley 4-1 in the League Cup," says Edwards. "Three of the goals had come in the last 20 minutes and I had had the temerity to describe it in print as a 'flattering victory.' Clough bounced over and gave me all sorts of grief: 'Hey, young man, I've won the European Cup twice, what gives you the right to describe my team as flattering?'

"Robbo was stood there with a big smirk on his face, trying his best not to laugh and not making a very good job of it. But then Cloughie turned to him. 'And you can put that fucking fag out,' he barked. You've never seen anyone move quicker. Robbo went white and stamped it out there and then. I found him later with his head in his hands. He groaned: 'I'm a grown man, I've been married and I've had kids. And I'm still frightened of him!'"

Clough may have sought psychological domination but he could also be like a sentimental favourite uncle. Robertson found himself engrossed by the manager's madman-or-genius show. He was captivated by the nuances of Clough's prickly persona as he fined players for the most minor infractions of the club dress code while at the same time pouring drink down their throats before important games.

"How exactly do you define charisma? The man was a genius. He didn't complicate the game like so many of these so-called coaches. And we were all in awe of him. Absolute awe.

"He used to call me a tramp and a wreck. Other times he would bet me he could go longer without a drink than I could without a cigarette. He would even phone me up sometimes to check what I was having for tea. 'I hope that's not bacon sizzling in the pan I can hear,' he'd say. He was obsessed with my lifestyle."

Clough may have scored the fastest 200 goals in the English game (219 games to be precise) but it was the quickness of his tongue that Robertson and his teammates were more concerned about.

"The classic one was when Tony Woodcock decided to grow a beard and the Gaffer asked what was on his face. Tony said that he just wanted to be different. The Gaffer told him if he wanted to be different, he should start by scoring a hat-trick.

"My mother used to get quite upset about some of the things he said about me but I can't speak highly enough of him. It was Martin who argued with him. Or Larry Lloyd. Me? I used to look forward to every Saturday. I just loved playing for him."

His teammates used to call him "teacher's pet." Certainly it is true that Clough grew remarkably fond of his number 11. When Trevor Francis, football's first £1million man, made his Forest debut Clough told him: "Don't worry about what to do, just give the ball to John Robertson and he'll do the rest . . . he's a better player than you."

In *Walking on Water*, Clough said: "If you think David Beckham is fairly handy with his right foot you should have seen the way Robbo crossed the ball with his left - or his right if need be."

"All I ever wanted was a 'well done' from him," says Robertson, who thought nothing of travelling down from Glasgow for both of Clough's memorial services. "He had this little hand signal where he put two fingers together in an 'O' shape. He would do that when I had done something well, and when he stepped out of the dug-out to do it . . . well, it would make me feel ten feet tall. I think he liked me as a player, Cloughie. And I loved the guy. Ultimate respect. There's Alex Ferguson, Bill Shankly and all the other legendary managers, but Clough has got to be the best of them all."

In later years, he and O'Neill plagiarised some of Clough's working practices. Like the time, on the eve of an important cup-tie for Wycombe, they referred back to the 1979 League Cup final against Southampton and plied their players with booze. O'Neill recalls: "All we got for it was a splitting headache and a six-goal thrashing."

That was one of few mistakes, however, in the O'Neill-Robertson managerial era, a path of near-unbroken success that has taken them from Grantham to Glasgow - and twice come close to moving into office at the City Ground.

In 1993 O'Neill had been the overwhelming favourite to replace Clough. When the job was offered, however, he wanted carte blanche to make wholesale changes to the backroom staff, starting off with bringing in Robertson. For reasons that remain wholly unconvincing, Forest's board asked him to reconsider and suggested he should work alongside Frank Clark. The directors then discovered why the 'O' in O'Neill is reputed to stand for 'obstinate', as he opted to stay at Wycombe Wanderers.

There was a horrible sense of déjà vu in the aftermath of Ron Atkinson's brief, and best-forgotten, spell in charge in 1999. O'Neill and Robertson were sorely tempted to leave Leicester (then in the Premiership) to take over at Forest (just relegated) only for another late volte-face.

The obvious question is 'why'? But for the first time Robertson clams up. "I don't think I should go into the details," he says. "Nah, let's leave that one there."

No matter. It can wait for another day, another book. Their reluctance to work with certain people at Forest should not dilute the appreciation and gratitude that is bestowed upon them.

# DEEP INTO THE FOREST

In April 1977 Robertson was in the Forest team beaten 1-0 at home by Cardiff City in the Second Division. He can reel off other defeats against Carlisle, Luton, Hull and Notts County. Yet just over two years later Forest had reached the pinnacle of European football and in 1980, on a sumptuous night in Madrid, his heroic contribution saw them overcome Hamburg to become only the eighth club after Real Madrid, Ajax, Bayern Munich, Liverpool, Benfica, Milan and Internazionale to win the European Cup more than once.

As a feat of over-achievement it is so staggering as to defy logical analysis. And how appropriate that it was Robertson, the mercurial Robertson, who should apply the finishing touch.

His eyes twinkle at the memory: the 21st minute, a one-two with Garry Birtles. "I was stretching but I caught it with the outside of my boot. I saw it head towards the corner. And then I thought: 'Wow, it's going in. It's actually going in.' It just crept inside the post and I couldn't believe it.

"You see other guys running to the supporters or doing somersaults when they score. I must have been in a state of shock. Or maybe I was just knackered - it had been a long run by my standards. I stood rooted to the spot, put my hands in the air and thought: 'Whoa there, I've just scored in the European Cup final.' When I was a kid the European Cup was for Puskas, Di Stefano, legends like that. And then I was mobbed, of course."